Delicious Jamaica!

Vegetarian Cuisine

Yvonne McCalla Sobers

Book Publishing Company
Summertown, Tennessee

Cover design: Sheryl Karas
Interior Design: Michael Cook

The Book Publishing Company
PO Box 99
Summertown, TN 38483

ISBN 1-57067-021-8

00 01 02 03   5 4 3 2

Sobers, Yvonne McCalla.
     Delicious Jamaica : vegetarian cuisine / Yvonne McCalla Sobers.
          p.   cm.
     Includes index.
     ISBN 1-57067-021-8 (alk. paper)
          1. Vegetarian cookery. 2. Cookery, Jamaican. I. Title.
     TX837.S677   1996
     641.5'636'097292--dc20   96-810
                                                                CIP

Calculations for the nutritional analyses in this book are based on the average number of servings listed with the recipes and the average amount of an ingredient if a range is called for. Calculations are rounded up to the nearest gram. If two options for an ingredient are listed, the first one is used. Not included are fat used for frying, unless the amount is specified in the recipe, optional ingredients, or servings suggestions.

Acknowledgments

I am grateful to

my African ancestors who passed on recipes by word of mouth

my Grandmother Clemmie McCalla and Annie Brown, who provided me with the smells, sights, and tastes of traditional Jamaican foods

my uncle Colin Brown who set an example of the vegetarian life-style, and who, nearing eighty years, maintains near-perfect health

Blossom Budhai and Maureen Rowe with whom I conducted classes in vegetarian cooking

Paul Johnson, nutritionist and president of the Vegetarian Society of Jamaica, who shared with me his research on vegetarianism in Jamaica

Janice White who introduced me to the Book Publishing Company

Bob Holzapfel and Michael Cook who guided me through all the stages of publishing

my sons, Pierre and Hilaire, my daughter-in-law Mechel, and all family and friends who sampled the recipes and offered suggestions to me.

Contents

INTRODUCTION

The Jamaican cook improvises on a given theme. The intuitive feel for quantities, taste, texture, and timing is passed on from one generation to another. The result of a strong oral tradition is that even today, an excellent cook might not be able to provide any more specific recipe directions than "A little of this, a toops (pinch) of that, and just enough of the other." Many of the measurements in this book arise from my own trial and error or are inspired by the data now available from recent writers who have sought to record traditional Jamaican recipes.

Jamaican foods reflect the global mix of those who lived here before Europeans entered this hemisphere, and those who came later with their artillery, their dreams, or their chains. The result is a culture in which Africa, Europe, and Asia are interwoven so closely that points of ethnic origin might be difficult to define.

I have sought to recognize the contributions of the different peoples to the development of the Jamaican cuisine. The categories are not intended to be exclusive or definitive; too much cross-fertilization has taken place over the last five centuries. For example, pepperpot originated with the Tainos, and that recipe (a stew with a long life) is still followed in parts of the Caribbean. However Jamaican pepperpot soup is more closely associated with an African soup. The method of jerking foods, adopted from the Tainos, was perfected by the Maroons—Africans who resisted slavery and set up independent communities in Jamaica.

Vegetarian substitutions have been made to replace meat, eggs, cow's milk, butter, refined sugar, and for the most part, rum or beer. The most frequent substitutions are:

  * tofu for protein such as meat or eggs
  * soymilk or coconut milk for cow's milk
  * vegetable oil for butter
  * honey, molasses, or brown sugar for refined sugar.

Some special aspects of Jamaican foods are the use of seasonings, spices, and coconut (grated or processed as milk, cream, or oil). The widespread use of coconut oil in Jamaica has not yet been linked to health problems. If you would prefer, other kinds of vegetable oil can be used instead of coconut oil, but you will lose some of the distinctive flavor.

Seasonings and spices can be varied according to taste. Black pepper, a favorite in Jamaican seasoning, is omitted for reasons of health. Fresh hot pepper is recommended, but dried hot pepper is an acceptable replacement. Fresh onion and garlic are generally preferred to the powdered equivalent.

The person on a slimming diet will need to watch for the oils and the sugars which are intrinsic to Jamaican foods. However, the range of seasonings, such as in jerk, can help to create interesting low-calorie meals. Grilling, where possible, can be used in place of frying, and steaming can be used in place of sautéing.

Jamaicans living abroad now report that Jamaican herbs, fruits, and vegetables are widely available in the major cities of Canada, the United Kingdom, and the United States of America. Many of these foods may also be found at other outlets for ethnic foods such as Greek or Hispanic food stores.

This book is organized to give you a historical/cultural perspective on Jamaican cuisine. In any event, the conventional way of organizing recipes, from appetizer to dessert, would not necessarily apply to the Jamaican tradition. Meals are not generally eaten in courses. A traditional breakfast can be as heavy as a midday meal. Sometimes soup is eaten as the main meal, and it may be followed by dessert. Appetizers are not usually expected, and dessert may be omitted after a heavy meal.

The chapters are arranged to include the primary ingredients and methods introduced or made popular by those who have influenced traditional Jamaican cooking:

The Tainos or Arawaks: corn, bread; barbecue

The Africans: coconut, ground corn, callalu (spinach), yam, peanut, ackee; thick soups and stews

The Spanish: beans, avocado, chocolate, banana, plantain; escabeche and frying

The British: mango, tamarind, breadfruit, wheat products; lighter stews, stuffed vegetables, patties, buns

The Indians and the Chinese: rice, Asian vegetables; curries and stir-fries

The Jews, Syrians, and Lebanese: eggplant, lentils, pita bread; kebab and some salads

The North Americans: fast foods, salads, and pasta

Granny's Kitchen: a compendium of favorite recipes including hot and cold drinks, porridge, main and side dishes, candies, and puddings.

GLOSSARY

Ackees: Boiled and tossed in seasoning, this vegetable is a special delicacy which came to Jamaica from Africa. Fresh ackees must be handled with care for the harvesting and cooking, but canned ackees are also available.

Annatto: These seeds give a rich orange-red color to soups and stews. The effect is similar to saffron.

Avocado: This fruit is eaten as a vegetable when ripe. The skin of a ripe avocado can be green, deep purple, or black. The most highly rated are the alligator and the Simmonds. The avocado pear originated in Mexico and was introduced by the Spanish to other parts of the world.

Bammy: This cassava bread was the staple food of the Arawaks and is produced in the southern region of Jamaica. Bammies are made as thick and large as a dinner plate or as thin and small as a saucer. Bammies are usually bought, rather than home made.

Bananas: The Spanish brought bananas to Jamaica from the Canary Islands. They are eaten green and boiled as a vegetable or ripe as a fruit. Ripe bananas will keep their color after you peel them if you sprinkle them with lime or lemon juice. The main varieties are the Lacatan, Robusta, and the prince of bananas, the Gros Michel.

Bissy: This nut is also called kola nut. It is grated and made into a tea which is used to aid digestion. This nut is widely used in West Africa and is an ingredient of cola drinks in North America .

Breadfruit: This plant was introduced by William Bligh whose crew mutinied on his famous ship, the Bounty. The breadfruit is a starchy vegetable with texture somewhat like bread. It is usually boiled or roasted over hot coals. You can also bake it in the oven. The most popular variety is the Yellow Heart breadfruit.

Bridal Wiss: This tree root is said to be rich in minerals and is taken to strengthen the nervous system.

Callalu: This plant is believed to be indigenous to Jamaica. In Jamaica it is called greens and is similar to spinach.

Cerasee: This herb is particularly bitter and is valued for as a cure for a range of physical complaints. It climbs on fences and grows wild.

Chainey root: This tree root, like bridal wiss, is said to be rich in minerals and is taken to strengthen the nervous system.

Cinnamon: The bark of a tree provides this spice, which is a vital ingredient in Jamaican chocolate, porridge, and pastries.

Chocolate: This is the name given to the drink made from cocoa beans. The cocoa beans are fermented, parched, pounded, and formed into balls, and this is called Jamaican cocoa.

Cho-cho: Cho-cho is also called chayote or Christophene. You can substitute cucumber or zucchini for this vegetable. It is shaped like a pear and absorbs flavor easily as it has no distinct taste of its own.

Cumin: This herb is a small dried seed which is integral to making curries.

Curry Powder: East Indians usually grind their own curry powder from a blend of spices, but you can look for high-quality, store-bought curry powder.

Dumplings: The traditional size of dumplings ranges from the little spinner to the large cartwheel which is flat and round. Soups and stews are not considered complete without dumplings.

Flour: Flour in these recipes refers to whole wheat flour.

Garden Cherry: This berry originates in the West Indies. It is small, bright red, and tart, and makes a delicious drink. It is very rich in Vitamin C.

Gingerroot: This is a root which is used to make drinks, season savory dishes, and spice up pastries and sweets. Jamaican gingerroot is of particularly high quality.

Molasses: Use molasses with caution as the taste can be overpowering. It gives a distinctive flavor to Jamaican lemonade and pastries, such as buns and gizzadas.

Ortanique: The name of this citrus fruit is taken from the words orange, tangerine, and unique. This delicious fruit is a cross between an orange and a tangerine and is unique to Jamaica.

Otaheite Apple: These apples are pear-shaped and dark on the outside and white on the inside. They are also available dried.

Peas: Jamaican red peas are also called red kidney beans. Gungo peas are also known as pigeon peas. Red peas and gungo peas are special favorites for making Rice and Peas (page 131) and Rich Stewed Peas (page 43). Gungo peas are a special favorite at Christmas time.

Papaya: Many folk myths surround this fruit which is generally referred to in Jamaica as pawpaw. It is linked to fertility as well as sterility.

Passion fruit: This round yellow-colored fruit grows on a vine. It provides pulp and seeds which are strongly flavored and tart. Passion fruit drink is heavenly.

Pepper: Jamaican soups and stews owe part of their distinctive flavor to the addition of a green (unripe) hot pepper. Cut hot peppers with a fork and a knife to avoid contact with your fingers. The hottest and most flavorful of Jamaican peppers is called the Scotch Bonnet.

Pimento: This spice is indigenous to Jamaica and is known to the rest of the world as allspice. The berry is said to combine the flavors of cinnamon, clove, pepper, and nutmeg. It is most often added to soups, stews, pickles, and jerk seasonings.

Plantain: This fruit resembles a very large banana. You can use it green, sliced and fried, or you can enjoy it ripe, fried, baked, boiled, or made into tarts.

Sarsaparilla: This tree root is believed to have blood cleansing properties. It is an ingredient of the North American drink, root beer.

Sauces

Hot Pepper Sauce: This sauce is also called Tabasco sauce, and you can use it instead of fresh hot pepper. Use it sparingly, especially if it originates in the Caribbean.

Pickapeppa Sauce: You can use vegetarian Worcestershire sauce as a replacement if you really cannot find this memorable Jamaican sauce.

Tamarind: The pulp of this fruit is dark brown and tart. The fruit can be eaten raw, preserved, or used to make a drink. It is available as a paste.

Wood roots: This is a combination of sarsaparilla, chainey root, and bridal wiss. The mixture is considered potent and is taken as a tonic.

Yam: This tuber originated in Africa and is popular among Jamaicans. It is not to be confused with the sweet potato. Yams are usually boiled or roasted, and the yellow variety is the most sought after.

THE TAINOS

The Tainos, generally referred to as Arawak Indians, are recorded as the original inhabitants of Jamaica. Christopher Columbus met them in 1494 when he was pursuing his claim that he had found a western route to the spices, gems, and perfumes of India. The Tainos were peaceful and easygoing; they did not long survive the Spanish insistence that they enrich the newcomers with land and labor, if not gold. These gentle people were extinct within a century of the arrival of the Spanish. They have left behind their rock carvings, their tools, and their foods.

Corn was a Taino staple, and today you will find roadside vendors in various parts of the Jamaican cities and countryside with boiled or roasted corn-on-the-cob.

The only bread the Taino knew was made from cassava, a fibrous root. Today, all over Jamaica you will find bammy, which is a flat cake made from cassava which has been grated, shaped, and toasted. Search Caribbean shops for this delicacy, and consider yourself lucky if you find bammies made in the Jamaican parish of St. Elizabeth. Finding this taste delight is worth the effort.

Another legacy of the Tainos is the art of barbecue. The Jamaican climate allows for year-round outdoor barbecues.

Heroes Circle Boiled Corn

Street vendors traditionally sell boiled and roasted corn on the sidewalks near National Heroes Park, formerly known as East Race Course, in Kingston.

6 ears corn
½ cup water
seasoning to taste
* salt

* hot pepper
* onion
* thyme

1. Remove the husks and silks from the corn. Retain a portion of the husk as a receptacle for the corn.

2. Bring the water to a boil in a heavy, covered pot.

3. Add the seasonings to the boiling water, and let simmer for about 5 minutes.

4. Add the ears of corn directly to the boiling water or to a steamer above the boiling water.

5. Bring to a rapid boil, reduce the heat, and simmer for about 7 minutes.

6. Remove the corn from the heat, place on enough of the husk to protect your fingers from the steam, lightly butter, and serve.

Serves 6

Per serving: Calories: 83, Protein: 2 gm., Fat: 0 gm., Carbohydrates: 17 gm.

Faith's Pen Roas' (Roasted) Corn

Faith's Pen is a point on the journey from Kingston to Ocho Rios and Montego Bay. Travelers usually stop here to treat themselves to Jamaican foods, including roasted corn.

Follow the recipe for boiled corn, and have a grill ready for use. Place the boiled corn on the grill for 3-5 minutes until the corn seems toasted.

Place the corn on the husk, and eat immediately. If it lies around, someone else will eat it for you.

Cassava Bammy

Bammies are a favorite food served with ackees, callalu, or Vegetable Run Down (page 32).

2 lbs. sweet cassava

1. Scrape the skin off the cassava, and finely grate them.

2. Squeeze out the juice from the grated cassavas, leaving a floury substance.

3. Rub through the cassava flour to remove all of the lumps.

4. Place a thick-bottomed pot over low heat. When the pot is hot, pour in the cassava flour, making a circle about 2 inches in diameter and about ½ inch thick.

5. When the bammy sets at the bottom, turn it over, and let the other side set.

6. Scrape if necessary to remove any scorched areas, then fry, steam or bake the following recipe.

Serves 2

Per serving: Calories: 134, Protein: 0 gm., Fat: 0 gm., Carbohydrates: 33 gm.

Fried Bammies

Bammies are usually made as a cottage industry, and Jamaican consumers usually purchase bammies in stores or markets. Vendors sell cooked bammies at Port Royal, which was once a haven for pirates; Hellshire Beach at Kingston Harbor, across the sea from Port Royal; and at Old Harbour Bay, which is about an hour's ride from Kingston.

2 store-bought bammies   **pinch of salt**
1-2 cups soymilk or coconut
   milk

1. Soak each bammy in a shallow bowl filled with milk for 10 minutes.

2. Fry or grill each bammy, whole, halved, or quartered until the bammy is light brown on all sides.

3. You can also lightly butter the bammies, and bake them for about 15 minutes in a 350°F oven. You may also grill or steam the buttered bammies for about 15 minutes until the flour is cooked.

Serves 2

Per serving: Calories: 173, Protein: 3 gm., Fat: 2 gm., Carbohydrates: 35 gm.

Xyamaca Barbecue Sauce

Xaymaca is the Taino word from which the name Jamaica is derived.

1 medium onion, chopped
2 cloves garlic, minced
⅓ cup oil
2½ cups tomato sauce
½ cup honey
1 tsp. salt

½ tsp. minced hot pepper
1 Tbsp. fresh parsley, chopped
1 bay leaf
4 pimento grains (allspice)
½ cup lemon juice
2 Tbsp. tamari

1. Sauté the onion and garlic in the oil until the onion is transparent.

2. Stir in the remaining ingredients, except the lemon juice and tamari, and simmer for about an hour.

3. Add the lemon juice and tamari, and simmer for another 10 minutes.

4. Remove the bay leaf and pimento grains (allspice), and serve

Serves 6

Per serving: Calories: 237, Protein: 2 gm., Fat: 11 gm., Carbohydrates: 32 gm.

Xaymaca Barbecued Tofu

The tofu replaces the meat the Arawaks hunted and ate.

1 lb. firm tofu
1 Tbsp. oil
¼ cup onions, chopped
2 cloves garlic, crushed and
    chopped
¼ tsp. hot pepper, seeded
    and chopped
¼ tsp. thyme
½ tsp. salt
2 Tbsp. tomato concentrate

½ cup water
¼ cup brown sugar or honey
¼ cup pineapple juice
1 Tbsp. lime or lemon juice
½ tsp. powdered ginger, or
    about ½-inch gingerroot,
    crushed or grated
1 Tbsp. prepared mustard
4 pimento grains (allspice)

1. Preheat the oven to 350°F.

2. Slice the tofu into ¼-inch slices, lightly fry, and set aside.

3. Sauté the onions, garlic, and hot pepper in the remaining oil, and blend with all the other ingredients until smooth.

4. Arrange the tofu slices in a baking dish, pour the sauce over the tofu, and bake for about 15 minutes.

Serves 4

Per serving: Calories: 179, Protein: 8 gm., Fat: 9 gm., Carbohydrates: 15 gm.

THE AFRICANS

Dr. Ivan Van Sertima, a historian of Caribbean origin, points out in his work <u>They Came Before Columbus</u> that Africans interacted with Amerindians before the Europeans arrived in the New World. The African presence in Jamaica is believed to have begun with African sailors who accompanied Columbus on his ships. The available documentation indicates African arrivals on board slave ships for about three hundred years after Columbus' visit. Africans came in captivity across the Atlantic to provide slave labor for plantations. Today, more than ninety per cent of the population of Jamaica is of African ancestry.

Africans who came to Jamaica originated mainly in West Africa—in particular the countries now known as Ghana and Nigeria. They brought to Jamaica drum rhythms and musical memories currently expressed as reggae. They also brought customs and speech patterns, which influence the way of life and the expression of language. And they introduced foods which are integral to Jamaican cuisine: yam, callalu, ground corn, ackee, and coconut oil—as well as modes of food preparation, in particular the thickening of soups and stews. Duckanoo, a steamed pudding, is the same in Jamaica as in Ghana.

Some common features in traditional kitchens are the mortar and pestle and the yabba which is a large, heavy earthenware bowl. The name and the method of making the bowl were brought to Jamaica by West Africans. Yabbas have been used for holding water, mixing batter, and cooking and serving food. The mortar and pestle are used for grinding such items as cocoa or coffee beans, plantains, and yams.

Jamaican yams, indigenous to Africa, are tuberous roots. They may be hard or soft, milky-white, or butter-yellow. Some yams still carry the African names such as Afu which means yellow in the Twi language of the Ashanti people of Ghana. What are commonly referred to in North America as yams are really sweet potatoes. If you really cannot find real yams in your supermarket or in a store that stocks African, Caribbean, or Latin-American foods, use regular potatoes instead.

Ackees, another name that comes from the Twi language, are part of the national dish of Jamaica. Ackees grow in many tropical countries but are eaten only in Jamaica. They are exported in cans, so you look for them in shops that sell Jamaican foods. Cooked ackees resemble scrambled eggs.

The Maroons were those of African descent who resisted enslavement and set up communities in the mountains of Jamaica. Their guerrilla tactics resulted in an eighteenth century treaty in which the British acknowledged the independence of the Maroons. These freedom fighters developed the "jerk" seasonings and method of food preparation, probably adapted from Arawak barbecue techniques.

The Maroons today keep alive the African traditions in music, dance, leadership, language, and general mores.

The wider Jamaican Community retains an African connection in
        *the dialect which mixes African words, grammar, and expressions
            with language forms from the Irish, Scottish, and English.
        *proverbs and fables, such as the Anansi stories
        *religious observances, such as pocomania, kumina, and myal
        *dances, such as dinkie-minnie, gerreh, and bruckins
        *international movements such as Garveyism and Rastfarianism.

The founder of Garveyism is the Honorable Marcus Mosiah Garvey, one of Jamaica's national heroes. Rastafarians revere the former Emperor of Ethiopia, Haile Selassie, who was also known as Ras Tafari, as the incarnation of God.

The African presence is experienced in many aspects of Jamaican life, and significantly in the foods.

Coconut Milk

1 dry coconut, with liquid you can hear inside when you shake the coconut

about 2 cups of water

Method A

1. Tap the coconut with a hammer to loosen the flesh inside.

2. Break open the coconut with the hammer, and use a strong knife to carefully remove the flesh inside. If you are using the grated coconut for pastry, peel off the brown tissue.

3. Grate the coconut into a bowl using the fine side of the grater, and cover with the water.

4. Use your hand to squeeze the grated coconut constantly for about 5 minutes.

5. Pour the mixture through a fine strainer or cheesecloth, squeezing tightly to extract as much of the liquid as you can.

Method B

1. Follow steps 1 and 2 of Method A.

2. Dice the coconut and place it in a blender or food processor with strong blades.

3. Add 2 cups hot water, and blend for 1-2 minutes until the mixture seems milky. Leave to cool slightly.

4. Pour the mixture through a cheesecloth, squeezing tightly to extract as much of the liquid as you can.

Method C

Choose the easier way by shopping for unsweetened frozen or canned coconut milk at a shop that stocks Asian, Hispanic, or Caribbean foods.

Do not make coconut milk from packaged coconut flakes or from commercial coconut cream, unless you want a sweet flavor.

Makes 2 cups

Per ¼ cup: Calories: 140, Protein: 1 gm., Fat: 12 gm., Carbohydrates: 3 gm.

Cornmeal Porridge

2 oz. cornmeal
1 pint water
pinch of salt
½ cup soymilk or coconut milk

⅓ cup water
¼ cup honey, or to taste
1 teaspoon vanilla
nutmeg and cinnamon to taste

1. Mix the cornmeal with just enough water to make a thick paste.

2. Bring the remainder of the water to a boil, and stir in the cornmeal paste and salt.

3. Continue cooking for about 7-10 minutes.

4. Mix the soymilk with an additional ⅓ cup water, and add the porridge.

5. Sweeten to taste and add the vanilla and spices.

Serves 4

Per serving: Calories: 126, Protein: 2 gm., Fat: 0 gm., Carbohydrates: 28 gm.

Duckanoo

This treat is also known as Tie-a-Leaf or Blue Drawers.

2 cups cornmeal
pinch of salt
¼ cup flour
½ tsp. mixed spice
½ tsp. cinnamon
1 cup coconut, grated
about 1½ cups soymilk or
   coconut milk

1½ tsp. molasses
¾ cup sugar
1 tsp. vanilla
banana leaves, cooking bags,
   or tin foil
banana bark or cord

1. Thoroughly blend all the dry ingredients and the grated coconut.

2. Mix together the soymilk, molasses, sugar, and vanilla.

3. Combine the dry and liquid ingredients, stirring briskly.

4. Place about ½ cup of the mixture into aluminium foil, blanched banana leaves, or cooking bags.

5. Package the mixture and tie with the banana bark or cord.

6. Place the parcels in enough boiling water to cover.

7. Cook for 40 minutes or until done.

Serves 4-6

Per serving: Calories: 583, Protein: 9 gm., Fat: 22 gm., Carbohydrates: 85 gm.

Turned Cornmeal

½ cup onions, chopped
2 scallions, chopped
¼ cup green peppers,
   chopped
½ cup tomatoes seeded,
   skinned, and chopped
1-2 cloves garlic (opt.)
1 Tbsp. oil
2 Tbsp. soymilk or coconut
   milk

½ cup cornmeal
1 hot pepper, finely chopped,
   or to taste
1 sprig of thyme
pinch of salt
pinch of pepper
4-6 okra, thinly sliced

1. Sauté the onions, scallions, green peppers, tomatoes, and garlic in the oil.

2. Pour the soymilk in a thick-bottomed saucepan.

3. Add the cornmeal, sautéed vegetables, hot pepper, thyme, salt, and pepper.

4. Cook over a low flame for about 30 minutes, stirring from time to time. Add the okra in the final 10 minutes.

5. Place the cooked cornmeal in a greased mould, and decorate with slices of sweet pepper and sprigs of parsley.

6. Turn out of the mould, and serve hot.

Serves 10

Per serving: Calories: 56, Protein: 1 gm., Fat: 2 gm., Carbohydrates: 9 gm.

Asham

1 cup dry corn grains   **3 Tbsp. brown sugar**

1. In a heavy pan, dry roast the corn for 10-15 minutes, stirring constantly, until the corn is dark brown and some of the grains have burst.

2. Place the corn in a blender, or in a mortar and pestle if you have the time to be traditional, and blend until the corn is powdery.

3. Sift the ground corn, add the sugar, and serve as a snack.

Serves 5

Per serving: Calories: 84, Protein: 1 gm., Fat: 0 gm., Carbohydrates: 20 gm.

Pepperpot Soup

3 cups of water, or 2½ cups water and ½ cup coconut milk
¼ cup callalu or spinach
2-3 bay leaves
6-8 pimento grains (allspice)
¼ carrot, sliced
¼ cup cho-cho, sliced
½ cup coconut, sliced

1 whole green hot pepper
1 large potato, diced
½ hot pepper, diced, or to taste
1 medium onion, diced
1 tsp. scallions, chopped
2 cloves garlic, crushed and chopped
1 sprig of thyme
salt to taste

1. Put the liquid in a saucepan, and bring to a rapid boil.

2. Add the callalu, bay leaves, pimento grains (allspice), carrot, cho-cho, coconut, whole green hot pepper, and potato, and cook until tender.

3. Stir and simmer for another 15 minutes.

4. Add the diced hot pepper, onion, scallions, garlic, thyme, and salt.

5. Stir and simmer for another 20 minutes.

Serves 4

Per serving: Calories: 185, Protein: 2 gm., Fat: 11 gm., Carbohydrates: 19 gm.

Creamy Pepperpot Soup

Follow all directions in Pepperpot Soup (page 27) through step 5, and continue as follows:

6. Remove the bay leaves and pimento grains (allspice),

7. Puree the soup in a blender.

8. Return to the pot and reheat if necessary.

9. Add ¼ cup plain yogurt, and serve immediately.

Serves 4

Per serving: Calories: 194, Protein: 3 gm., Fat: 11 gm., Carbohydrates: 20 gm.

Steamed Callalu

salt to taste
about ½ cup water
6 cups callalu leaves, stripped
    of fiber and chopped
1 oz. butter or margarine

½ cup scallions or onions,
    chopped
1 tsp. hot pepper, chopped
2 small tomatoes, seeded,
    skinned, and chopped

1. Place the salt and water in a saucepan, and bring to a boil.

2. Add the callalu and simmer for 10-12 minutes until the leaves are tender but still green, and drain.

3. Melt the butter and sauté the scallions and hot pepper.

4. Add the tomatoes and cook until the tomatoes are tender.

5. Add the callalu, toss well, and serve.

Serves 6

Per serving: Calories: 55, Protein: 1 gm., Fat: 3 gm., Carbohydrates: 3 gm.

Callalu Run Down

12 young okra, topped, tailed, and sliced

6 cups callalu leaves, stripped of fibre and chopped

2 or 3 cooking tomatoes, seeded, skinned, and chopped

½ cup scallions or onions, chopped

1 tsp. hot pepper, seeded and chopped

1 Tbsp. sweet pepper, seeded and chopped

1 or 2 cloves garlic, crushed and chopped

1 sprig thyme

1 cup water

1 cup coconut milk

1 oz. butter or margarine

1. Place the okra, callalu, tomatoes, scallions, hot pepper, sweet pepper, garlic, and thyme in a saucepan.

2. Add the water and coconut milk, and boil until the okra and callalu are tender but still have their color.

3. Toss with butter and serve.

Serves 6

Per serving: Calories: 171, Protein: 3 gm., Fat: 13 gm., Carbohydrates: 10 gm.

Yam Run Down Casserole

1 lb. yams
2 medium carrots
1 onion, chopped
salt to taste
1 Tbsp. sweet pepper, seeded and chopped
1 tsp. hot pepper, seeded and chopped

1 sprig thyme
6 pimento grains (allspice)
2 cloves garlic, crushed and chopped
3 medium tomatoes, skinned, seeded, and chopped
1 cup coconut milk

1. Peel, wash, and boil the yams until firm and tender.

2. Preheat the oven to 350°F.

3. Slice the yams and carrots.

4. Mix together the onion, salt, sweet pepper, hot pepper, thyme, pimento grains (allspice), and garlic.

5. Grease a pyrex dish and place in it alternating layers of yams, carrots, tomatoes, and seasoning mix.

6. Cover the ingredients with coconut milk, and bake until done.

Serves 4-6

Per serving: Calories: 254, Protein: 3 gm., Fat: 10 gm., Carbohydrates: 35 gm.

Vegetable Run Down

4 cups coconut milk
1 cup green beans, sliced
2 medium carrots, sliced
½ cup tomatoes, skinned,
    seeded, and chopped
1 whole, unripe hot pepper
1 medium clove garlic,
    crushed and chopped
4 pimento grains (allspice)

¼ tsp. thyme
¼ tsp. hot pepper, chopped
1 small head of cauliflower,
    separated into chunks
1 sprig celery, sliced
½ cup bean sprouts
¼ cup onions, finely chopped
6 okra, sliced

1. Simmer the coconut milk in a heavy pan until the milk begins to turn oily (about an hour).

2. Add the green beans, carrots, tomatoes, whole hot pepper, and seasonings.

3. Simmer for 10 minutes and add the rest of the vegetables.

4. Simmer for another 10 minutes, remove the whole hot pepper, and serve with boiled potatoes or rice.

Serves 6

Per serving: Calories: 419, Protein: 4 gm., Fat: 34 gm., Carbohydrates: 17 gm.

Peanut Stew

½ cup ground peanuts or
   crunchy peanut butter
1 cup vegetable stock
1 cup water
1 cup onions, sliced
2 cloves garlic, crushed and
   chopped
½ tsp. hot pepper, chopped

2 Tbsp. oil
salt to taste
¼ tsp. thyme
2 bay leaves
2 cups canned tomatoes
1 whole, unripe hot pepper
6 okra, sliced

1. Blend the peanut butter, stock, and water.

2. Sauté the onions, garlic, and chopped hot pepper in the oil, combine with the seasonings, canned tomatoes, whole hot pepper, and peanut stock, and simmer for 20 minutes.

3. Add the okra and simmer for another 5 minutes, or until the okra are tender and firm.

4. Recheck the seasonings and adjust if necessary.

5. Remove the whole hot pepper, and serve over rice.

Serves 4-6

Per serving: Calories: 177, Protein: 5 gm., Fat: 11 gm., Carbohydrates: 12 gm.

Peanut Soup

1 medium onion, chopped
2 cloves garlic, crushed and
  chopped
¼ tsp. hot pepper, seeded
  and chopped
1 Tbsp. oil
2 cups ground peanuts or
  peanut butter
1 cup coconut milk or water

2 cups vegetable stock
½ tsp. salt
2 bay leaves
6 pimento grains (allspice)
2 scallions, crushed whole
1 whole hot pepper, unripe
6 okra, sliced
¼ tsp. dried thyme

1. Sauté the onion, garlic, and chopped hot pepper in the oil until the onion is transparent.

2. Add the ground peanuts, coconut milk, vegetable stock, salt, bay leaves, pimento grains (allspice), scallions, and whole hot pepper.

3. Bring to a boil and simmer for an hour, skimming off the excess oil.

4. Add the okra and thyme, and simmer until the okra is tender and firm. Correct the seasonings and serve hot.

Serves 6

Per serving: Calories: 420, Protein: 13 gm., Fat: 33 gm., Carbohydrates: 15 gm.

Ackee Heritage

2 cans ackees
1 small onion, sliced
1 sweet pepper, sliced
¼ tsp. hot pepper, seeded
  and chopped
1 scallion, chopped
1 Tbsp. coconut oil
1 small tomato, skinned,
  seeded, and chopped

¼ tsp. dried thyme
salt to taste
1 Tbsp. texturized vegetable
  protein, soaked in 1 Tbsp.
  warm water and squeezed dry
  (opt.)

1. Drain the canned ackees.

2. Sauté the onion, sweet pepper, hot pepper, and scallion in the oil until the onion is transparent.

3. Add the tomato and thyme, and simmer until the tomato is tender.

4. Add the ackees and texturized vegetable protein, tossing lightly to ensure that the ackees are covered in the sauce.

5. Simmer for about 3 minutes, and serve hot with Johnny Cakes (page 57), Fried Plantains (page 53), Baked Breadfruit (page 68), or boiled yams or potatoes.

Ackee Tart

Follow the recipe for Ackee Heritage, and use as filling for tarts. Top the tarts with whole wheat bread crumbs, and bake.

Ackee and Tofish

Follow the recipe for Ackee Heritage. Replace the texturized vegetable protein with ½ lb. tofu which has been frozen, thawed, squeezed dry, soaked in salt water overnight, and squeezed dry again.

Jerk Seasoning (dry)

2 Tbsp. onion powder
½ tsp. garlic powder
2 tsp. ground thyme
1½ tsp. salt
¼ tsp. ground nutmeg

½ tsp. ground cinnamon
2 tsp. brown sugar
1½ tsp. powdered hot pepper
1 tsp. ground pimento (allspice)

Combine all the ingredients and store in an airtight jar.

Makes about ⅓ cup

Per tsp.: Calories: 21, Protein: 0 gm., Fat: 0 gm., Carbohydrates: 5 gm.

Jerk Seasoning (moist)

1 large onion, finely chopped
4 scallions, finely chopped
1 hot pepper, very finely
    chopped
2 tsp. honey
2 Tbsp. tamari
1 Tbsp. cider vinegar

2 Tbsp. coconut oil
1 tsp. salt
½ tsp. ground nutmeg
½ tsp. ground cinnamon
½ tsp. ground dried thyme
1 tsp. ground pimento (allspice)

Combine all the ingredients in a blender or food processor, blend until smooth, and store refrigerated in an air tight jar.

Makes about 1 cup

Per Tbsp.: Calories: 20, Protein: 0 gm., Fat: 1 gm., Carbohydrates: 2 gm.

Jerk Tofu

2 lbs. tofu, sliced and lightly poached
¼ cup Jerk Seasoning (moist) (page 37)

About ½ cup barbecue sauce or tomato sauce

1. Marinate the tofu in the jerk seasoning for two hours or overnight if possible.

2. Preheat the oven to 350°F.

3. Cover with barbecue sauce and bake for about 15 minutes, or cook the marinated tofu over hot coals for about 5 minutes, basting with the sauce.

4. Serve hot with Rice and Peas (page 131), plain rice, or baked potatoes.

Serves 6

Per serving: Calories: 134, Protein: 11 gm., Fat: 6 gm., Carbohydrates: 5 gm.

Jerk Potatoes

3 large potatoes
1-2 Tbsp. oil
1-2 Tbsp. Jerk Seasoning (dry)
   (page 36)

½ cup water or vegetable
   stock
fresh parsley, chopped for
   garnish

1. Steam the potatoes until tender, and cut them into cubes.

2. Heat the oil in a skillet. Stir in the Jerk Seasoning, then add the potatoes and water.

3. Cook until the water evaporates, and the mixture is dry.

4. Stir in the chopped parsley, and serve.

Serves 3-4

Per serving: Calories: 193, Protein: 2 gm., Fat: 5 gm., Carbohydrates: 33 gm.

Jerk Steamed Vegetables

Follow the recipe for Jerk Potatoes, but substitute yams, broccoli, cauliflower, pumpkin, or cabbage, for the potatoes.

Jerk Potato Stir

3 large potatoes
½ lb. tofu, poached
1-2 cloves garlic, crushed and finely chopped
¼ cup fresh parsley, finely chopped
¼ cup sweet pepper, seeded and finely chopped

¼ - ½ cup liquid from the boiled potatoes
1 Tbsp. tamari
1 tsp. Jerk Seasoning (dry or moist) (pages 36 & 37)
¼ tsp. dried thyme

1. Steam the potatoes until tender, drain, reserving the liquid, and cut into cubes. Cut the poached tofu into cubes.

2. Combine the tofu, potatoes, garlic, parsley, and sweet pepper, and toss lightly.

3. Heat the liquid from the boiled potatoes, and add the tamari, Jerk Seasoning, and thyme.

4. Simmer the mixture for about a minute, then add the potato mix. Toss lightly and cook until all the liquid is absorbed. Serve hot.

Serves 4

Per serving: Calories: 166, Protein: 6 gm., Fat: 2 gm., Carbohydrates: 29 gm.

THE SPANISH

Christopher Columbus established colonial contact between Europe and Jamaica. Conquest and counter-conquest brought about cultural clashes which left beliefs in the superiority of some races, their color, language, religion, and ultimately their food.

Spain is remembered in place names such as Puerto Seco, Rio Minho, Montego (a corruption of manteca, meaning lard) Bay and Ocho Rios (a corruption of las chorreras, meaning waterfalls). Discovery Bay is the point at which Columbus landed, and Runaway Bay the area from which the Spanish settlers fled the British conquerors.

The Spanish brought beans, citrus, chocolate, avocados, the marinated or escabeche method, the frying of foods—for which they needed lard—and coconut tarts, which are called gizzadas. They also introduced guavas, bananas, and pineapples.

Stewed Peas

1½ cups red peas (red kidney beans)
2 cups water
2 cups coconut milk
2 bay leaves
6 pimento grains (allspice)
2 whole medium cloves garlic
1 whole, unripe hot pepper
¼ tsp. hot pepper, chopped
2 scallions
½ cup onions, chopped
¼ tsp. thyme
1 clove garlic, crushed and chopped

1. Cover the peas with cold water, and soak overnight.

2. In a saucepan, place the peas, soaking liquid, coconut milk, bay leaves, pimento grains (allspice), whole garlic, whole hot pepper, and scallions.

4. Bring slowly to a boil, and simmer for about 2 hours, or until the peas are tender.

5. Add the onions, thyme, and crushed garlic, and simmer for another 20 minutes.

6. Adjust the seasonings if necessary. Thicken the stew by blending about 1 cup of the stew and returning the purée to the saucepan.

7. Remove the scallions, bay leaves, and hot pepper, and serve hot with rice.

Serves 6

Per serving: Calories: 319, Protein: 9 gm., Fat: 18 gm., Carbohydrates: 28 gm.

Stewed Gungo or Pigeon Peas

Use gungo or pigeon peas instead of red peas or red kidney beans.

Rich Stewed Peas

Add about ½ lb. tofu that has been frozen, thawed, squeezed dry, and cubed, to the saucepan in the final 20 minutes.

Serves 6

Per serving: Calories: 347, Protein: 11 gm., Fat: 19 gm., Carbohydrates: 29 gm.

Pea Soup

8 oz. red peas, red kidney beans, gungo peas, or pigeon peas
4 cups water
2 cups coconut milk
2 bay leaves
6 pimento grains (allspice)
1 whole, unripe hot pepper
1 onion, chopped
1 whole clove garlic
2 carrots, chopped
1 potato, cubed
½ lb. yellow yams, cubed
1 small sweet potato, cubed
2 scallions, crushed whole
¼ tsp. hot pepper, seeded and chopped
1 clove garlic, chopped
1 tsp. salt
½ tsp. dried thyme

1. Wash the peas and soak a few hours or overnight.

2. Add enough water to the soaked peas to make 4 cups. Add the coconut milk, bay leaves, and pimento grains (allspice).

3. Cook for about 2 hours until the peas are almost tender. Add the whole hot pepper, half the onion, the whole garlic, carrots, potato, yams, sweet potato, scallions, and chopped hot pepper.

4. Cook for another 20 minutes, or until the peas are tender and the vegetables are cooked.

5. Add the rest of the onion, chopped garlic, salt, and thyme. Correct the seasonings to taste, and simmer for another 10 minutes.

6. Puree half of the soup to thicken, and serve hot.

Serves 6

Per serving: Calories: 420, Protein: 9 gm., Fat: 18 gm., Carbohydrates: 53 gm.

Escabeche Tofu

1 lb. firm tofu, cubed
salt to taste
⅓ cup flour for coating tofu
oil for frying
1 tsp. hot pepper, seeded and
    chopped
¼ cup onion, sliced
¼ cup green sweet peppers,
    sliced

½ cup red sweet peppers, sliced
2 bay leaves
4 pimento grains (allspice)
1 Tbsp. oil
⅔ cup cider vinegar
1¼ cups water

1. Season the tofu with the salt, coat with the flour, and fry until brown on all sides. Remove from the frying pan, and drain the tofu on paper towels.

2. Combine all the other ingredients in a saucepan, and bring to a boil.

3. Simmer for about 10 minutes until the onions are cooked, and remove from the heat. Remove the bay leaves and pimento grains (allspice).

4. Pour the liquid on the tofu, and serve hot, or allow the tofu to steep for 12 hours, and serve cold.

Serves 4

Per serving: Calories: 167, Protein: 9 gm., Fat: 8 gm., Carbohydrates: 13 gm.

Simmonds Pear (Avocado) Sauce

In Jamaica, the Simmonds avocado is sought for its flavor, size, and appearance. Any other variety of avocado can be substituted in this recipe.

2 avocados, peeled and chopped

2 large tomatoes, skinned, seeded, and chopped

1 tsp. hot peppers, seeded and chopped

1 medium onion, finely chopped

1 clove garlic, crushed and chopped

½ tsp. lime or lemon juice

2 Tbsp. fresh parsley, finely chopped

1. Place all the ingredients in a blender, and purée until smooth.

2. Serve with a salad, on crackers, or as a dip.

Serves 8

Per serving: Calories: 106, Protein: 1 gm., Fat: 6 gm., Carbohydrates: 10 gm.

Country-Style Chocolate

¾ cup country-style
   chocolate or baking
   chocolate, grated
3 cinnamon sticks

6 cups soymilk or coconut milk
pinch salt
⅓ tsp. grated nutmeg
honey to taste

1. Place the chocolate, cinnamon sticks, and soymilk in a pan with a thick bottom.

2. Bring to a boil and simmer for about 15 minutes.

3. Pour the liquid through a fine strainer, then add the salt, nutmeg, and honey.

4. Reheat if necessary and serve hot.

Serves 6

Per serving: Calories: 229, Protein: 7 gm., Fat: 13 gm., Carbohydrates: 20 gm.

Gizzada

Short cut pastry dough:
3 oz. margarine or butter
1 cup flour
½ Tbsp. brown sugar
about 2 Tbsp. cold water
Filling:
¾ cup coconut, grated
½ cup brown sugar
½ tsp. cinnamon
¼ tsp. ground ginger
¼ tsp. grated nutmeg
1 tsp. vanilla or almond extract
2 tsp. water
1 tsp. molasses
¼ tsp. lime juice

1. Preheat the oven to 400°F.

2. To make the short cut pastry; rub the margarine into the flour, add ½ Tbsp. brown sugar, 2 Tbsp. cold water, and mix.

3. Roll out the dough ½ inch thick.

4. Cut the pastry into 3-inch circles, and fit into shallow patty tins.

5. In a bowl, mix together the coconut, ½ cup brown sugar, cinnamon, ginger, and nutmeg.

6. Combine the dry and liquid ingredients, stir well, and place a little filling in each patty case.

7. Bake for about 15 minutes until the pastry is golden brown.

Makes 12 gizzadas

Per serving: Calories: 216, Protein: 2 gm., Fat: 14 gm., Carbohydrates: 20 gm.

Lacatan Banana Loaf

Lacatan and Gros Michel are popular types of bananas in Jamaica. The Gros Michel is considered particularly tasty.

1 cup soft tofu (½ lb.), crumbled
2 cups bananas, mashed
1 Tbsp. lime or lemon juice
rind of 1 lime, grated
1 tsp. vanilla
¼ cup honey
½ cup oil
2 cups whole wheat or unbleached flour

1½ tsp. baking soda
¼ tsp. cinnamon
¼ tsp. ground ginger
¼ tsp. ground nutmeg
1 cup dried tropical fruit (such as dried papaya, pineapple, or otaheite apple)
¼ cup cashews, chopped

1. Preheat the oven to 350°F.

2. In a blender, combine the tofu, bananas, lime juice and rind, vanilla, honey, and oil, and purée until smooth.

3. Sift together the flour, baking soda, and add the spices.

4. Combine the dry and liquid ingredients, then add the dried fruit and cashews.

5. Pour the batter into a well-greased 9-inch baking tin or loaf pan, and bake until a toothpick comes out clean, about 50 minutes.

6. Cool in the pan for 5 minutes, then remove the loaf.

Makes 12 slices

Per serving: Calories: 291, Protein: 5 gm., Fat: 13 gm., Carbohydrates: 37 gm.

Gros Michel Baked Bananas

1 cup Jamaica rum or cider
1 Tbsp. lime juice
½ tsp. ground cinnamon
¼ tsp. nutmeg

2 Tbsp. honey
½ tsp. molasses
4-6 bananas

1. Preheat the oven to 350°F.

2. Place the rum in a saucepan with the lime juice, cinnamon, nutmeg, honey, and molasses. Bring to a boil, stirring continually, lower the heat, and simmer for 5 minutes.

3. Slice the bananas and place them in a baking dish.

4. Pour the sauce over the bananas, and bake until the bananas are tender, about 20 minutes. Serve cold.

Serves 4-6

Per serving: Calories: 238, Protein: 1 gm., Fat: 0 gm., Carbohydrates: 31 gm.

St. Mary Banana Fritters

The Jamaican parish of St. Mary is the region in which mainly bananas are grown.

3 medium ripe bananas
1 tsp. lime juice
6 Tbsp. whole wheat flour
1½ tsp. baking powder
½ tsp. grated nutmeg

¼ cup soymilk
2 Tbsp. honey
1 egg or egg replacer
brown sugar
lime or lemon slices

1. Mash the bananas and lime juice until smooth.

2. Sift together the flour, baking powder, and nutmeg.

3. Combine the soymilk with the honey and a lightly beaten egg.

4. Add the liquid to the dry ingredients, tossing lightly to make a batter.

5. Drop the batter by tablespoon in hot oil, and fry until the fritters are brown.

6. Drain on crushed paper towels, sprinkled with brown sugar, and serve with slices of lime or lemon.

Serves 12

Per serving: Calories: 58, Protein: 1 gm., Fat: 0 gm., Carbohydrates: 12 gm.

Fried Green Plantains

2 large green plantains
2 cups water

1-2 tsp. salt
oil for frying

1. Remove the skin and slice the plantains in rounds about ½ inch thick.

2. Mix the water with the salt, and soak the plantains for about an hour. Drain and pat dry.

3. Fry the slices in a skillet on both sides for a few moments over medium heat. Do not allow the slices to brown.

4. Remove the slices from the skillet. On a sheet of waxed paper, roll each slice with a rolling pin until the slice is flattened.

5. Return to the skillet and fry in hot oil until the slices are brown and crisp.

Serves 3-4

Per serving: Calories: 125, Protein: 1 gm., Fat: gm., Carbohydrates: 29 gm.

Fried Ripe Plantains

2 plantains, ripe and firm
oil for frying

flour or whole wheat bread
crumbs for coating (opt.)

1. Remove the skin and slice the plantain lengthwise or in rounds about ¼ inch thick.

2. Dip in flour or bread crumbs, and fry in hot oil until the plantain slices are brown.

Plantain Chips

2 green plantains
2 cups water

1-2 tsp. salt
coconut oil for frying

1. Remove the skin and slice the plantains very thin.

2. Soak the plantain slices in salted water for about an hour. Drain and pat dry.

3. Fry the slices quickly in hot oil until the slices are golden brown.

4. Drain and serve.

Banana Chips

Follow the recipe for plantain chips, replacing the plantains with 4-5 green bananas.

Plantain Tarts

short crust pastry rolled into
    rounds (page 48)
3 very ripe plantains, peeled
pinch of salt

nutmeg to taste
½ tsp. almond extract
½ cup brown sugar

1. Preheat the oven to 400°F.

2. Parboil the plantains in slightly salted water.

3. Remove the membranes and seeds, and crush until no lumps remain.

4. Add the nutmeg, almond extract, and brown sugar. Add a little water if the mixture seems dry.

5. Fill half the pastry round. Fold into a crescent shape, and seal the edges.

6. Bake the tarts for about 40 minutes, or until the tarts are golden brown.

Serves 12

Per serving: Calories: 120, Protein: 1 gm., Fat: 2 gm., Carbohydrates: 22 gm.

THE BRITISH

Oliver Cromwell sent soldiers and sailors to challenge the right of Spain to occupy all the New World. In Jamaica, the British encountered little resistance from the Spanish, who packed up and departed in haste.

The British ruled Jamaica from 1655 to 1962 when the island recovered its independence. The British heritage contributed the language, the customs of the governing classes, and a tradition of presumed superiority of imported foods.

British sailors such as Captain Bligh (of Mutiny on the Bounty fame) introduced to Jamaica such crops as mango and tamarind from India, as well as otaheite apple and breadfruit from the Pacific islands. Look for these items in shops specializing in ethnic foods.

The British contributed chips, pies, relatively light stews, stuffed vegetables, pastries, puddings, wheat products, and in particular a sweet bread, which is called bun, to Jamaican cuisine. Bun and cheese are particularly popular at Easter time. Patties are favorite snack items and may have links to Cornish pasty which is also a round pastry filled, folded, sealed, and baked.
Johnny Cakes are said to have been originally called Journey cakes; and Stamp and Go is believed to be taken from the language of British sailors.

Spinners

(small dumplings)

1 cup flour   **water for mixing**
¼ tsp. salt

1. Sift the flour and salt.

2. Add enough water to form a firm dough.

3. Roll the dough into shapes 1 inch long and ¼ inch thick. Drop into soup or stew about 15 minutes before cooking is completed.

Serves 6

Per serving: Calories: 67, Protein: 2 gm., Fat: 0 gm., Carbohydrates: 14 gm.

Johnny Cakes

1½ cups flour
1 tsp. baking powder
¼ tsp. salt

1 oz. margarine
about ½ cup water
1 cup oil

1. Sift the flour, baking powder, and salt.

2. Rub in margarine

3. Bind with water to form a soft dough. Add more water if needed.

4. Divide the dough into 10 balls, and knead each ball from the outside in for half a minute.

5. Fry the balls in hot oil. As the lower half browns, turn each cake over, and cook gently until done.

6. Drain and serve hot.

Makes 10 cakes

Per cake: Calories: 176, Protein: 2 gm., Fat: 12 gm., Carbohydrates: 13 gm.

Stuffed Johnny Cakes

Follow the recipe for Johnny Cakes through step 4, then flatten the balls, and fill them with leftover vegetables. Fold the dough over the vegetables, seal the edges, and fry.

Makes 10 cakes

Per stuffed cake: Calories: 186, Protein: 2 gm., Fat: 12 gm., Carbohydrates: 15 gm.

Stuffed Vegetable Patties

Patty Filling:
2 cloves garlic, crushed and
   chopped
½ cup onions, chopped
½ tsp. hot pepper, seeded
   and chopped
1 Tbsp. oil
1 cup bread crumbs
1 tsp. salt
2 cups cooked cabbage,
   pumpkin, callalu, mixed
   vegetables, or 2 cups
   cooked and mashed split

peas, lentils, pigeon peas or
   red kidney beans, or 2 cups
   texturized vegetable protein,
   soaked in 2 cups hot water
   for 10 minutes and squeezed
1 tsp. paprika
½ tsp. thyme
Patty Dough:
2 cups flour
½ tsp. salt
1 cup margarine
1 cup cold water

1. Sauté the garlic, onions, and hot pepper in the oil until the onion is transparent.

2. Add the bread crumbs and then the rest of the ingredients. Sauté for another 10 minutes. Set aside.

3. Preheat the oven to 400°F.

4. To make the patty dough, sift the flour and salt.

5. Rub in the margarine.

6. Bind with water to form a firm dough, and knead for 2 minutes.

7. Roll out thinly and cut into circles.

8. Place filling on one half of the circle, fold to cover with the other half, and seal the edges.

9. Bake until lightly browned.

Makes 10 patties

Per patty with filling: Calories: 346, Protein: 7 gm., Fat: 19 gm., Carbohydrates: 35 gm.

Stamp and Go

½ lb. tofu, frozen, thawed, and squeezed dry (opt.)
½ medium onion, finely chopped
2 scallions, chopped
1 hot pepper, seeded and finely chopped
¼ cup tomatoes, skinned, seeded, and chopped
2 cloves garlic, crushed and finely chopped
1½ cups whole wheat flour
1 tsp. baking powder
1½ cups cornmeal
about ½ tsp. salt
½ tsp. dried thyme
water
oil for frying

1. Soak the tofu about 2 hours or overnight in lightly salted water. Squeeze dry again and finely chop before using.

2. Sauté the onion, scallions, hot pepper, tomatoes, and garlic until the onion is transparent.

3. Sift together the flour and baking powder, and add the cornmeal, salt, thyme, and sautéed vegetables.

4. Add enough water to make a soft sticky batter.

5. Drop the mixture by spoonfuls into hot oil in a shallow skillet.

6. Fry until the fritters are golden brown, drain in crushed kitchen paper, and serve hot.

Serves 4-6

Per serving: Calories: 321, Protein: 11 gm., Fat: 3 gm., Carbohydrates: 61 gm.

Ben Johnson Vegetable Stew

Ben Johnson Day is the day of the week, frequently Friday, when not much food is in the house, and a visit to the market is due. It's a real test of the imagination to produce a meal from the bits and pieces left in the pantry.

3 potatoes, or ½ lb. yams
½ lb. pumpkin
1 cho-cho (opt.)
1 small turnip
1 onion, chopped
2 cloves garlic, crushed and
    chopped
2 stalks celery, chopped
¼ tsp. hot pepper, seeded
    and chopped
1 sweet pepper, chopped
2 Tbsp. butter
2 Tbsp. mustard

1-2 Tbsp. molasses
3 Tbsp. tamari
2 cups stock, or 1 cup stock and
    1 cup Red Stripe Beer
2 medium tomatoes, skinned,
    seeded, and chopped
4 pimento grains (allspice)
1 tsp. basil
¼ tsp. thyme
1 bay leaf
1 whole, unripe hot pepper
salt to taste
¼ cup fresh parsley, chopped

1. Scrub and trim the potatoes, or peel and wash the yams, quarter lengthwise, and slice in ½-inch slices.

2. Slice the pumpkin, cho-cho, and turnip the same thickness as the potatoes, and steam these vegetables with the potatoes.

3. Sauté the onion, garlic, celery, hot pepper, and sweet pepper in the butter until the onion is transparent.

4. Mix the mustard, molasses, tamari, and stock.

5. In a saucepan, combine the sauce, steamed vegetables, sautéed vegetables, tomatoes, pimento grains (allspice), basil, thyme, bay leaf, and whole hot pepper.

6. Simmer for 10 minutes, add the salt and parsley, and thicken the sauce by cooking uncovered for another 5 minutes. Serve with rice or whole-grain noodles.

Serves 6

Per serving: Calories: 170, Protein: 3 gm., Fat: 5 gm., Carbohydrates: 28 gm.

Okra Stew

Follow the directions for Vegetable Stew through step 6, and add 5 okra, that have been topped, tailed, and sliced, before simmering the stew.

Serves 6

Per serving: Calories: 183, Protein: 3 gm., Fat: 5 gm., Carbohydrates: 30 gm.

String Bean Stew

Slice 1 lb. string beans lengthwise and steam with the other vegetables.

Serves 6

Per serving: Calories: 230, Protein: 5 gm., Fat: 8 gm., Carbohydrates: 34 gm.

Crunchy Stew

Follow the directions for Vegetable Stew through step 7, and add ¼ cup unsalted chopped almonds or cashews before thickening the stew.

Serves 6

Per serving: Calories: 206, Protein: 4 gm., Fat: 8 gm., Carbohydrates: 29 gm.

Lucea Shepherds Pie

Lucea yams are soft, white, and similar in texture to a white potato.

2 cups leftover mashed Lucea yams, or 3 medium potatoes, ¼ cup soymilk, and ½ tsp. salt
1 pound broccoli or cauliflower
1 onion, chopped
2 cloves garlic, chopped
¼ tsp. hot pepper, seeded and chopped
1 Tbsp. oil
4 medium carrots, diced
1 sweet pepper, diced

2 stalks celery, diced
½ pound snow peas, sliced lengthwise (opt.)
¾ cup fresh tomatoes, skinned, seeded, and chopped, or ¼ cup tomato paste and ½ cup water
1 bay leaf
4 pimento grains (allspice)
½ tsp. basil
¼ tsp. thyme
¼ cup bread crumbs
¼ tsp. paprika

1. If you don't have leftover mashed potatoes, cook the potatoes, and mash them with the soymilk and salt.

2. Cut the broccoli into florets and the stems in bite-sized pieces.

3. Preheat the oven to 350°F.

4. Sauté the onion, garlic, and hot pepper in the oil until the onion is transparent.

5. Add the broccoli, carrots, sweet pepper, celery, and snow peas, and toss well.

6. Add the tomatoes, bay leaf, and pimento grains (allspice), bring to a boil, and turn down the heat. Cover and simmer until the vegetables are firm and tender, about 15 minutes. Add the basil and thyme, and mix well.

7. Put the vegetables in a 9 x 13-inch baking dish. Spread the potatoes over the top, and sprinkle with the bread crumbs and paprika.

8. Bake the pie for 10-15 minutes until the potatoes are hot. Serve at once.

Serves 6

Per serving: Calories: 157, Protein: 4 gm., Fat: 2 gm., Carbohydrates: 28 gm.

Lentil Shepherds Pie

Replace the broccoli or cauliflower with mashed lentils or other leftover beans.

Serves 6

Per serving: Calories: 251, Protein: 10 gm., Fat: 2 gm., Carbohydrates: 45 gm.

Tofu Shepherds Pie

Add ½ lb. tofu, that has been frozen, thawed, and squeezed dry, to the cooked vegetables.

Serves 6

Per serving: Calories: 186, Protein: 6 gm., Fat: 4 gm., Carbohydrates: 29 gm.

Hot and Spicy Shepherds Pie

Add 1 Tbsp. (or less) of pickapeppa sauce to the seasonings.

Serves 6

Per serving: Calories: 157, Protein: 4 gm., Fat: 2 gm., Carbohydrates: 28 gm.

Ital Cornbread

Ital refers to the Rastafarian way of cooking without salt. This cornbread also contains the Rastafarian colors—red, yellow, and green.

¼ cup flour
1 tsp. baking powder
1 tsp. honey or brown
   sugar
pinch of salt (opt.)
1 cup cornmeal
1 egg or egg replacer
4 tsp. melted margarine or
   butter

½ cup skim milk
1 Tbsp. scallions
1 Tbsp. sweet red pepper, seeded
   and chopped
1 Tbsp. sweet green pepper,
   seeded and chopped

1. Preheat the oven to 425°F.

2. Sift the dry ingredients together.

3. Stir in the lightly beaten egg, margarine, and milk using light, rapid strokes, then add the scallions, red pepper, and green pepper.

4. Bake for 25 minutes in a greased 8-inch-square tin.

Serves 5

Per serving: Calories: 177, Protein: 5 gm., Fat: 5 gm., Carbohydrates: 28 gm.

Brawta Bread Pudding

Brawta, in Jamaican creole, means a little extra. You will ask for brawta after your first slice of bread pudding, especially if you included the Jamaican rum in the mixture.

2 cups soymilk
½ cup honey
2 oz. Jamaica rum (opt.)
¼ lb. tofu, or 1 egg
1 tsp. vanilla
¼ tsp. each: nutmeg, cinnamon, and ground ginger

4 oz. bread in slices or small pieces
¼ cup raisins
¼ cup dried tropical fruit mix, pineapple, carambola, papaya, citrus peel
1 ripe banana, sliced (opt.)
½ oz. butter or margarine

1. Preheat the oven to 325°F

2. Blend together the soymilk, honey, rum, tofu, vanilla, and spices.

3. Grease a 5 x 7 x 2-inch baking dish. Alternate layers of bread and fruit, beginning and ending with bread.

4. Pour the liquid over the ingredients in the baking dish, and bake until set, about 45 minutes. Serve hot or cold.

Serves 6

Per serving: Calories: 231, Protein: 6 gm., Fat: 5 gm., Carbohydrates: 41 gm.

Plantation Muffins

Sugar was the base of Jamaica's economy in the 17th and 18th centuries. The molasses, ginger, and cinnamon in these muffins recreate a sense of the old-style sugar plantation.

2 cups flour	**½ cup firm tofu**
½ tsp. salt	**¾ cup water**
1 tsp. baking powder	**2 Tbsp. oil**
¾ tsp. baking soda	**1½ Tbsp. honey**
½ tsp. cinnamon	**2 tsp. molasses**

1. Preheat the oven to 350°F.

2. Mix the flour, salt, baking powder, baking soda, and cinnamon.

3. Blend the tofu, water, oil, honey, and molasses until smooth.

4. Fold the liquid ingredients into the dry ingredients until they are just moistened.

5. Fill oiled muffin tins ¾ full.

6. Bake for 15-20 minutes or until golden brown.

Makes 12 muffins

Per muffin: Calories: 107, Protein: 3 gm., Fat: 2 gm., Carbohydrates: 17 gm.

Stuffed Cho-Cho

3 cho-chos
1 medium onion, chopped
⅛ tsp. hot pepper, finely
   chopped
¼ cup sweet pepper, seeded
   and chopped

1 Tbsp. butter or oil
1 cup bread crumbs or leftover
   rice
1 tsp. salt
½ cup fresh parsley, chopped
2-3 Tbsp. plain yogurt (opt.)

1. Preheat the oven to 350°F.

2. Cut the cho-chos in half lengthwise, and remove the seeds.

3. Boil the cho-chos in salted water for about 25 minutes or until cooked.

4. Remove the inside from the cho-cho halves, leaving the shells.

5. Sauté the onion, hot pepper, and sweet pepper in the butter.

6. Mash the cho-cho insides, add to the sautéed onion and peppers, and mix with the remaining ingredients.

7. Place a portion of stuffing in each cho-cho shell.

8. Bake until the stuffing is light brown, about 20 minutes.

Serves 4-6

Per serving: Calories: 95, Protein: 2 gm., Fat: 3 gm., Carbohydrates: 14 gm.

Baked Breadfruit

Breadfruit for boiling is less mature than breadfruit used for baking or roasting. Ask advice from the vendor if you are not sure how to choose a breadfruit for baking.

1 breadfruit, selected for baking (not boiling)   **1 Tbsp. coconut oil**

1. Preheat the oven to 400°F.

2. Oil the breadfruit well and bake for about 1 hour or until tender and firm.

3. Remove the skin and core. Slice and serve as a replacement for baked potatoes or bread.

Serves 2

Per serving: Calories: 176, Protein: 2 gm., Fat: 6 gm., Carbohydrates: 27 gm.

Stuffed Yellow Heart Breadfruit

Yellow Heart breadfruit is particularly tasty, but any type of breadfruit will do.

1 Baked Breadfruit (page 68)
1 medium onion, finely
   chopped
1 clove garlic, crushed and
   chopped
1 scallion, chopped
1 sweet pepper, seeded and
   chopped

1 Tbsp. coconut oil
1 tomato, skinned, seeded, and
   chopped
¼ tsp. hot pepper, seeded and
   finely chopped
½ tsp. salt

1. Remove the core of the breadfruit, but leave the skin intact.

2. Sauté the onion, garlic, scallion, and sweet pepper in the oil until the onion is transparent. Add the tomato and cook for another 5 minutes.

3. Preheat the oven to 350°F.

4. Scoop out the flesh of the breadfruit, and finely chop or mash. Combine all the ingredients, stuff into the breadfruit shell, cover with foil, and bake until thoroughly heated.

Serves 2

Per serving: Calories: 227, Protein: 3 gm., Fat: 6 gm., Carbohydrates: 38 gm.

Variation: The breadfruit can also be stuffed with Ackee Heritage (page 35) or your favorite stuffing.

Breadfruit Fries

1 Baked Breadfruit (page 68)   **coconut oil for frying**

1. Remove the core and the skin of the breadfruit.

2. Slice the remainder of the breadfruit no more than ½ inch thick.

3. Fry until the slices are crisp and golden brown. Serve in place of French fries.

Serves 2

Per serving: Calories: 236, Protein: 2 gm., Fat: 13 gm., Carbohydrates: 27 gm.

Easter Bun

1 Tbsp. active dry yeast
½ cup honey
1 cup warm water
4½ cups unbleached flour
½ cup oil
1 tsp. salt
2 Tbsp. orange rind, grated
2 oz. mixed citrus peel, finely
    chopped
1 Tbsp. molasses

1 tsp. each: ground cinnamon,
    nutmeg, and ginger
4 oz. raisins
4 oz. currants
½ tsp. each: ground fennel and
    caraway seeds
Glaze:
2 Tbsp. honey
1 tsp. lime juice

1. Dissolve the yeast in 1 Tbsp. honey and 1 cup warm water, and let stand for 5 minutes.

2. Mix in 2 cups of flour and another 3 Tbsp. honey.

3. Combine well and let rise until the mixture doubles.

4. Blend together the oil, salt, and the remainder of the honey, and add to the yeast mixture, using your hands.

5. Add the remainder of the flour a little at a time.

6. Knead for about 10 minutes or until the dough is smooth and not too soft or too stiff.

7. Add the rest of the ingredients, and knead until they are evenly mixed through the dough.

8. Let the dough rise until double again.

9. Preheat the oven to 350°F.

10. Make loaves to half fill the baking tins, and let the dough rise to the edge of the tins. Bake for 45 minutes or until golden brown.

11. Brush with oil about 5 minutes before removing from the oven.

12. Heat the honey and lime juice, and glaze the buns with this mixture while they are cooling.

Makes 24 slices

Per slice: Calories: 174, Protein: 3 gm., Fat: 4 gm., Carbohydrates: 31 gm.

Quick Bun

1½ oz. oil
½ cup honey
1 egg or egg replacer
½ cup stout
1½ cups unbleached flour
1 tsp. baking powder

½ tsp. mixed spice
½ tsp. cinnamon
4 Tbsp. raisins
4 Tbsp. currants
2 Tbsp. mixed citrus peel, finely chopped

1. Preheat the oven to 350°F.

2. Blend together the oil, honey, egg, and stout until the mixture is smooth.

3. Sift together the flour, baking powder, and spices. Add the liquid ingredients, raisins, currants, and citrus peel, and mix well.

4. Place the mixture in a 9 x 4-inch loaf tin, and bake for 45 minutes or until done.

Serves 10

Per serving: Calories: 172, Protein: 3 gm., Fat: 5 gm., Carbohydrates: 29 gm.

Tropical Gingerbread

4 oz. oil
½ cup honey
½ cup molasses
1 egg or egg replacer
⅔ cup soymilk, coconut milk,
    or orange juice
2 cups unbleached flour

1 tsp. baking soda
2 tsp. ground ginger
1 tsp. ground cinnamon
½ cup raisins or dried tropical
    fruit (such as dried pineapple
    or dried banana)

1. Preheat the oven to 325°F.

2. Blend together the oil, honey, molasses, egg, and soymilk until the mixture is smooth.

3. Sift together all the dry ingredients.

4. Add the liquid and the dried fruit to the dry ingredients, and mix well.

5. Place the mixture in a greased 9 x 4-inch loaf pan, and bake for about 70 minutes until done.

Makes 12 slices

Per slice: Calories: 265, Protein: 3 gm., Fat: 10 gm., Carbohydrates: 42 gm.

THE INDIANS AND CHINESE

Slavery officially ended in Jamaica in 1838. The British were concerned that people of African ancestry would no longer provide the free labor needed to enrich and sustain the British Empire. Indentured laborers were therefore brought from India and China to meet the demand for workers on sugar estates.

This new wave of immigrants brought with them their vegetables and fruits such as pak-choi and lychee; their foods such as roti, noodles, and rice; and their cooking techniques such as curry, sweet and sour, and stir-fry.

Jamaican curries tend to be oilier and spicier than East Indian curries. They are usually patterned on the cooking style of Madras which is the area of India from which most of the immigrants originated.

For similar reasons, Chinese cooking in Jamaica is influenced by the Cantonese style.

Curry Powder

Jamaican ginger, much of it grown on the plains of Clarendon, is of particularly high quality.

8 oz. coriander seeds
4 oz. cumin seeds
2 oz. fennel seeds
2 oz. fenugreek seeds
4 oz. cardamoms
4 oz. turmeric powder

2 oz. pimento grains (allspice)
2 oz. cloves
2 oz. ground ginger
2 oz. cinnamon
1 tsp. nutmeg powder
1 tsp. chili powder

1. Roast the coriander, cumin, fennel, and fenugreek separately.

2. Peel the cardamoms, then grind all the seeds, and mix with the powders.

Note: Coriander and the cumin are the most essential spices. Experiment with the other spices until you find the blend that suits you.

Makes 4 cups

Per Tbsp.: Calories: 35, Protein: 1 gm., Fat: 1 gm., Carbohydrates: 5 gm.

Island Curry Sauce

1 whole clove garlic
2 Tbsp. oil
½ cup onions, sliced
2 scallions
1 tsp. hot pepper, seeded and
    chopped
2-3 cloves garlic, crushed and
    chopped
1 tsp. lime or lemon juice
½ cup coconut milk

1-3 Tbsp. curry powder
¼ cup tomato paste
1½ cups water
1 whole, unripe hot pepper
1-2 tsp. salt
¼ tsp. thyme
1 tsp. honey
2 Tbsp. soy sauce
1 Tbsp. cornstarch

1. In a heavy saucepan, sauté the whole clove of garlic in 1 Tbsp. of oil until the garlic turns brown, and discard the garlic.

2. Add the remainder of the oil, and sauté the onions, scallions, hot pepper, and chopped garlic until the onions are transparent.

3. Combine the lime juice, coconut milk, and curry powder, and add to the saucepan, stirring constantly until the ingredients are mixed.

4. Mix the tomato paste with the water, and add to the saucepan together with the whole pepper. Simmer for about 20 minutes, stirring occasionally.

5. Add the salt and thyme, and adjust the seasonings.

6. Combine the honey, soy sauce, and cornstarch with enough water to make a runny paste, add to the saucepan, and stir constantly until the sauce thickens.

7. Remove the whole hot pepper before serving.

Serves 6-8

Per serving: Calories: 99, Protein: 1 gm., Fat: 7 gm., Carbohydrates: 6 gm.

East West Curry Sauce

1 clove garlic, crushed
1½ medium onions, minced
3 Tbsp. oil
1 tsp. gingerroot, grated
1 Tbsp. curry powder
2 Tbsp. whole wheat flour

1 cup vegetable stock or water
1 Tbsp. honey
2 Tbsp. tamari
2 Tbsp. tomato sauce
8 oz. yams or potatoes, diced
4 oz. pumpkin, diced

1. Sauté the garlic and onions in the oil until the onions are transparent.

2. Add the gingerroot, curry powder, and flour. Cook for about 1 minute, stirring constantly.

3. Stir in the vegetable stock, honey, tamari, and tomato sauce.

4. Add the potatoes and pumpkin, and simmer for about 30 minutes, stirring occasionally until the vegetables are tender. Serve over steamed vegetables.

Serves 6

Per serving: Calories: 144, Protein: 2 gm., Fat: 7 gm., Carbohydrates: 19 gm.

Vegetable Curry

¼ pound string beans
3 medium carrots
3 medium potatoes
2 cho-chos or medium zucchini
2 Tbsp. oil
1 tsp. black mustard seeds
½ cup onion, chopped
½ tsp. hot pepper, seeded
   and chopped

1 clove garlic, crushed and
   chopped
1 tsp. turmeric powder
1 tsp. curry powder
1 cup coconut milk
1 bay leaf
1 tsp. salt
juice of 1 lemon or lime

1. Cut the string beans, carrots, potatoes, and cho-chos into strips.

2. Heat the oil in a heavy pot with a lid. Add the mustard seeds and cover until the seeds stop popping.

3. Sauté the onion, hot pepper, and garlic, and then add the rest of the spices.

4. Add the sliced vegetables, except the zucchini, and stir to coat with the spices, seasonings, and oil.

5. Add the coconut milk and bay leaf, cook until the vegetables are almost done, then add the zucchini.

6. When the vegetables are cooked, add the salt, turn off the heat, and add the lemon juice.

Serves 6

Per serving: Calories: 226, Protein: 3 gm., Fat: 10 gm., Carbohydrates: 23 gm.

Jamdown Curry

Jamdown is a name for Jamaica, sometimes used in the vernacular.

¼ pound string beans
3 medium carrots
3 medium potatoes
½ lb. pumpkin

1 cup peas
2 cups Island Curry Sauce
(page 77)

1. Steam the vegetables and the peas separately.

2. Add the Curry Sauce, toss the vegetables to coat with the sauce, heat fully, and serve.

Serves 6

Per serving: Calories: 177, Protein: 4 gm., Fat: 5 gm., Carbohydrates: 28 gm.

Dal 1845

The first East Indians landed in Jamaica in 1845.

1 cup split peas
1 whole clove garlic
½ tsp. gingerroot, grated
2 bay leaves
4 pimento grains (allspice)
1 whole hot pepper
2 scallions, whole and crushed
1 tsp. curry powder
4 cups boiling water

¼ tsp. thyme
1 medium onion, chopped
1 clove garlic, crushed and chopped
½ tsp. hot pepper, seeded and chopped
3 Tbsp. oil
1 tsp. ground cumin

1. Place the split peas in a saucepan with the whole clove of garlic, gingerroot, bay leaves, pimento grains (allspice), whole hot pepper, scallions, and curry powder.

2. Cover with boiling water and simmer until the split peas are tender. Add the thyme in the last 5 minutes of cooking time.

3. Pour off the excess liquid, remove the whole hot pepper, scallions, bay leaves, and pimento grains (allspice), and mash the split peas into a purée.

4. Sauté the onion, remaining garlic, and chopped hot pepper in the oil until the onion is transparent. Add the cumin and mix well.

5. Add the mashed split peas, heat through, and serve.

Serves 4-6

Per serving: Calories: 178, Protein: 6 gm., Fat: 9 gm., Carbohydrates: 20 gm.

Curried Callalu

2 scallions, chopped
¼ cup sweet pepper, seeded
and chopped
1 tsp. oil
2 cups callalu, lightly steamed
2 medium potatoes, lightly
cooked and diced

½ cup fresh corn
¼ tsp. thyme
1 tomato, skinned, seeded, and
chopped
1-1½ cups of Island Curry
Sauce (page 77)

1. Lightly sauté the scallions and sweet pepper in the oil.

2. Add all the other ingredients, and simmer for about 5 minutes, stirring occasionally to prevent sticking. Serve immediately.

Serves 4-6

Per serving: Calories: 141, Protein: 3 gm., Fat: 5 gm., Carbohydrates: 21 gm.

Seasoned Rice (Pilaf)

2 Tbsp. oil
2 large onions, sliced
1 clove garlic, crushed and
    chopped
¼ tsp. hot pepper, seeded and
    chopped
½ cup carrots, chopped
2 cups cashews, chopped
1½ cups brown rice

2 bay leaves
4 pimento grains (allspice)
1 whole, unripe hot pepper
4 cloves
1 tsp. salt
½ tsp. gingerroot, chopped
4 cups water or vegetable stock
¼ cup fresh parsley, chopped

1. Heat the oil in a heavy saucepan with a lid, and lightly sauté the onions, garlic, hot pepper, carrots, and cashews.

2. Add the rice and sauté for another 3 minutes.

3. Add the bay leaves, pimento grains (allspice), whole hot pepper, cloves, salt, gingerroot, and water. Bring to a boil and simmer for about 45 minutes, or until the rice is tender.

4. Remove the whole pepper, stir in the parsley, and serve hot.

Serves 6-8

Per serving: Calories: 419, Protein: 9 gm., Fat: 23 gm., Carbohydrates: 44 gm.

Spice Rice

2 Tbsp. oil
1 large onion, sliced
¼ tsp. hot pepper, seeded
   and chopped
½ pound pumpkin, peeled
   and cubed
2 tsp. curry powder
½ tsp. turmeric

1½ cups brown rice
2 bay leaves
1 tsp. salt
1 whole, unripe hot pepper
4 cups water or vegetable stock
Garnish:
onions, fried
sprigs of fresh parsley

1. Heat the oil in a heavy saucepan with a lid, and sauté the onion, chopped hot pepper, and pumpkin.

2. Add the curry powder, turmeric, and brown rice, and sauté for another 3 minutes.

3. Add the bay leaves, salt, whole hot pepper, and water, bring to a boil, and simmer for about 45 minutes, or until the rice is tender.

4. Garnish with fried onions and parsley.

Serves 4-6

Per serving: Calories: 259, Protein: 5 gm., Fat: 6 gm., Carbohydrates: 46 gm.

Number Eleven Mango Chutney

They are called Number Eleven Mangos because they were the eleventh of about 18 varieties imported into Jamaica in the middle of the nineteenth century. The Number Eleven is a common mango with a distinctive flavor.

5 cups firm ripe mangoes, diced
2 cups raisins
¼ cup gingerroot, finely chopped
¾ cup onion, chopped

1 cup sweet peppers, chopped
½-1 Tbsp. hot peppers, finely chopped
1 tsp. salt
3 cups brown sugar
2½ cups cider vinegar

1. Place all the ingredients in a heavy pot.

2. Bring to a boil, stirring occasionally.

3. Simmer for 30 minutes until the mixture is thick.

4. Cool for 15 minutes, stir vigorously, and bottle.

Makes 12 cups

Per ¼ cup: Calories: 85, Protein: 0 gm., Fat: 0 gm., Carbohydrates: 21 gm.

Mr. Yap's Stir Fry Vegetables

My daughter-in-law's grandfather, Mr. Yap, introduced the Chinese way of life to a mountain side Jamaican village. He settled in this village after his period of indentured servitude ended.

4 cups of vegetables, chosen from carrots, broccoli, cauliflower, cabbage, pak choi, snow peas, mushrooms, bean sprouts
½ cup celery
½ cup sweet pepper
¼ cup scallions, chopped

2 Tbsp. oil
1 whole clove garlic
1 onion, chopped
1 clove garlic, chopped
1 tsp. gingerroot, minced
½ cup water
½ Tbsp. tamari
1 Tbsp. cornstarch

1. Cut the vegetables into attractive shapes: diagonals or sticks.

2. Heat the oil in a wok or skillet, fry the whole garlic until it is brown, and discard the garlic.

3. Stir-fry the onion then add the chopped garlic and gingerroot.

4. Add all the vegetables, starting with those that take longer to cook and ending with the bean sprouts and the scallions.

5. Combine the water with the tamari and cornstarch in a small bowl.

6. Add this mixture to the stir-fried vegetables, tossing until the sauce thickens, and all the vegetables are coated. Serve at once.

Serves 4-6

Per serving: Calories: 103, Protein: 2 gm., Fat: 5 gm., Carbohydrates: 11 gm.

Madame's Sweet and Sour Sauce

Many Chinese established community shops after they ceased to be indentured. The Chinese wife of the shop owner was usually referred to as Madam.

1 Tbsp. oil
1 clove garlic, crushed
1 small onion, thinly sliced
1 sweet pepper, thinly sliced
2 oz. mushrooms
¼ cup pineapple chunks

1 Tbsp. honey
3 Tbsp. cider vinegar
½ cup water or vegetable stock
2 Tbsp. tamari
½ tsp. gingerroot, grated

1. Heat the oil in a large frying-pan or wok.

2. Add the garlic and onion, and stir-fry for 2 minutes.

3. Add the sweet pepper, mushrooms, and the remaining ingredients, and mix together.

4. Cook, stirring constantly, until thick.

Serves 4-5

Per serving: Calories: 73, Protein: 1 gm., Fat: 3 gm., Carbohydrates: 10 gm.

Barry Street Chow Mein

Many of the Chinese storekeepers and traders set up establishments on Barry Street in Kingston.

¼ lb. dry Chinese noodles
2 tsp. oil
½ cup scallions, chopped
1 Tbsp. gingerroot, finely shredded
¼ tsp. hot pepper, chopped
½ cup sweet pepper, seeded and chopped
½ cup celery, seeded and chopped
3 medium carrots, cut into thin sticks
1 cup bean sprouts
¼ tsp. salt
1 Tbsp. tamari

1. Boil the noodles until just tender, and drain.

2. Heat the oil in a wok or a skillet, and sauté the scallions, gingerroot, hot pepper, sweet pepper, celery, carrots, and bean sprouts.

3. Add the salt and then the noodles.

4. Add the tamari, mix everything thoroughly, and serve immediately.

Serves 4-6

Per serving: Calories: 265, Protein: 7 gm., Fat: 11 gm., Carbohydrates: 32 gm.

Veggy Fried Rice

2 Tbsp. oil
2 whole cloves garlic
2 medium onions, chopped
2 cloves garlic, crushed and
    finely chopped
1 cup celery, chopped
½ cup sweet peppers,
    chopped

½ cup carrots, coarsely grated
4 cups cold, cooked rice
1 cup bean sprouts
2 scallions, chopped
1-2 Tbsp. tamari
2 tsp. pickapeppa sauce (opt.)
fresh parsley, chopped

1. Heat the oil in a heavy saucepan with a cover, and fry the whole cloves of garlic until they are brown. Remove the garlic.

2. Sauté the onions and chopped garlic until the onion is transparent. Then add the celery, sweet peppers, and carrots, and sauté another 2 minutes.

3. Add the cooked rice, continue stir-frying for another 3 minutes, and then add the bean sprouts and scallions.

4. Add the tamari and pickapeppa sauce, and mix well for another minute. Serve hot, garnished with chopped parsley.

Serves 6

Per serving: Calories: 233, Protein: 5 gm., Fat: 6 gm., Carbohydrates: 41 gm.

THE JEWS, SYRIANS, AND LEBANESE

People from the Middle East came to Jamaica seeking opportunities for trade. Portuguese Jews arrived with Christopher Columbus, but Syrian and Lebanese merchants settled in Jamaica after slavery ended. These groups are still well represented in business, but their influence on foods is not significant. Jewish cuisine is not generally known in Jamaica, but the Jews are believed to have introduced the eggplant to Jamaica. Syrian pita bread is popular and readily available.

Peppery Tabouli

⅓ cup bulgur wheat
⅔ cup water
½ cup mint leaves, chopped
2 cups fresh parsley, finely
   chopped
½ cup celery, finely chopped
1½ cups tomato, skinned,
   seeded, and chopped

2 small cucumbers, finely
   chopped
½ cup scallion, finely chopped
½ cup lime juice
1 tsp. salt
½ cup olive oil
½ tsp. hot pepper, chopped
lettuce leaves

1. Soak the bulgur wheat in the water for 10 minutes, and drain.

2. Mix all the ingredients, except the lettuce leaves.

3. Cover and store in the refrigerator for 12-24 hours.

4. Toss the salad so that all ingredients are well mixed.

5. Check the seasonings and serve the salad on a bed of lettuce.

Serves 6-8

Per serving: Calories: 198, Protein: 2 gm., Fat: 14 gm., Carbohydrates: 13 gm.

Tropical Lentil Soup

2 cups uncooked lentils
8 cups water or vegetable
   stock
1 onion, chopped
1 clove garlic, crushed and
   chopped
¼ cup scallions, chopped
2 carrots, chopped
1 small cho-cho, peeled,
   seeded, and chopped
   (opt.)

½ cup celery, chopped
½ lb. yam or potato, chopped
2 bay leaves
1 whole, unripe, hot pepper
1½ tsp. salt
2 Tbsp. olive oil
2 tsp. cider vinegar
½ cup fresh parsley, chopped

1. Pick rocks and sticks from the lentils, and wash.

2. Mix all the ingredients, except the vinegar and parsley, in a heavy saucepan, and cook until the lentils are very soft, about an hour.

3. Stir in the vinegar and parsley, remove the whole hot pepper, and serve hot.

Serves 6-8

Per serving: Calories: 233, Protein: 12 gm., Fat: 5 gm., Carbohydrates: 37 gm.

Stuffed Pita Bread

1 Tbsp. lime or lemon juice
2 Tbsp. olive oil
1 clove garlic, crushed and
   finely chopped
½ tsp. pickapeppa sauce
1 tomato, skinned, seeded,
   and chopped
½ cup scallions, finely
   chopped

½ tsp. hot pepper, finely
   chopped
¼ tsp. basil
1 cup alfalfa sprouts
¼ cup cucumber, peeled and
   finely chopped
2 Tbsp. fresh parsley, chopped
4 whole wheat pitas, cut in
   halves

1. Combine all the ingredients, reserving some of the sprouts.

2. Fill the pita pockets with the mixture, and top with sprouts.

Serves 4

Per serving: Calories: 227, Protein: 7 gm., Fat: 8 gm., Carbohydrates: 32 gm.

Kebabs

8-10 cherry tomatoes
10-15 button mushrooms
1 small cauliflower
2 medium cucumbers
2 medium onions
10-12 small potatoes, lightly
   cooked, or 8 thick slices of
   roasted or boiled breadfruit
½ lb. firm tofu

⅔ cup oil
3 Tbsp. lime juice or cider
   vinegar
½ tsp. dry mustard
¼ tsp. paprika
½ tsp. dried basil
pinch powdered garlic
pinch powdered hot pepper

1. Wash and dry the uncooked vegetables.

2. Break the cauliflower into large florets, cut the cucumber into 1 inch slices, and peel the onions and cut them into thick wedges.

3. Halve the potatoes or cut the breadfruit into chunks.

4. Poach the tofu, drain, dry, and cut into cubes.

5. Arrange the ingredients on about 12 skewers.

6. Blend the oil, lime juice, mustard, paprika, basil, garlic, and hot pepper, and brush the kebabs with this dressing.

7. Grill the kebabs for about 10 minutes under or over medium heat. Turn frequently and continue to baste with the dressing.

8. Remove from the heat when the kebabs are slightly brown and becoming tender. Serve hot with pita bread.

Makes 12 kebabs

Per kebab: Calories: 202, Protein: 3 gm., Fat: 12 gm., Carbohydrates: 21 gm.

Falafels

2 cups cooked chick peas
⅓ cup water
¼ cup whole wheat bread
   crumbs
1 Tbsp. whole wheat flour
1 medium onion, finely
   chopped
2 cloves garlic, crushed and
   chopped
¼ cup fresh parsley or
   coriander leaves, chopped
½ tsp. salt
¼ tsp. hot pepper, finely
   chopped
½ tsp. cumin

½ tsp. ground turmeric
¼ tsp. dried basil
flour for coating
oil for frying
½ cup onion, chopped
⅛ tsp. salt
1 Tbsp. lemon juice
½-1 cup plain yogurt or soft tofu
6 whole wheat pitas, halved
1 tomato, skinned, seeded, and
   chopped
1 cup lettuce
½ cup bean sprouts

1. Grind the chick peas in a grinder or food processor.

2. Add the water, bread crumbs, flour, onion, garlic parsley salt, hot pepper, cumin, turmeric, and basil.

3. Form the mixture into small balls, coat with the flour, and fry the balls in the oil until they are light brown. Drain on crushed paper towels.

4. Blend the onion, salt, lemon juice, and yogurt.

5. Serve the falafel in pita halves with the tomatoes, lettuce, bean sprouts, and yogurt dressing.

Serves 6

Per serving: Calories: 293, Protein: 13 gm., Fat: 4 gm., Carbohydrates: 52 gm.

Eggplant Dip

1 medium eggplant
1 Tbsp. tahini
1 medium onion, minced
2-3 cloves garlic, crushed and
    minced

juice of ½ lime or lemon
salt to taste
1 Tbsp. olive oil
½ tsp. cumin, ground

1. Roast, bake, or steam the eggplant until it is soft but still firm.

2. Peel and mash the cooked eggplant, or chop it in a blender or food processor.

3. Add the tahini, onion, garlic, lime juice, and salt, and let stand for about 30 minutes.

4. Mix in the oil and cumin just before serving.

Serves 6

Per serving: Calories: 72, Protein: 1 gm., Fat: 3 gm., Carbohydrates: 9 gm.

Eggplant Cutlets

1 medium eggplant
flour for coating

oil for frying
sauce of your choice

1. Slice the eggplant.

2. Add salt to the eggplant, place the slices in a glass bowl, and put a weight on the eggplant to draw off the fluid, which may be bitter

3. Leave for about half an hour, and the pour off the liquid.

4. Dry the eggplant slices with kitchen towels.

5. Coat the eggplant slices with flour, and shake off the excess.

6. Heat the oil in a frying pan, and deep fry the eggplant slices until they are light brown and done all through.

7. Drain off the excess oil on crushed kitchen paper. Serve hot with the sauce of your choice.

Serves 3-4

Per serving: Calories: 167, Protein: 3 gm., Fat: 8 gm., Carbohydrates: 22 gm.

Hummus

1 cup cooked chick-peas
about 6 Tbsp. chick-pea liquid
salt to taste
3 Tbsp. lime or lemon juice
1-2 cloves garlic, minced

3 Tbsp. tahini
1 tsp. olive or sesame oil
paprika
fresh parsley

1. Place in a blender, the chick peas, chick-pea liquid, salt, and lime juice, and blend until smooth.

2. Add the garlic and tahini, and mix well.

3. Refrigerate for about 1 hour.

4. Garnish with the oil, paprika, and parsley, and serve with crackers or toasted pita bread.

Serves 6

Per serving: Calories: 102, Protein: 3 gm., Fat: 5 gm., Carbohydrates: 10 gm.

NORTH AMERICA

The connection between Jamaica and North America has grown stronger in post-colonial times. Many Jamaicans have migrated to the U.S.A. and Canada in search of economic improvement, and the Jamaican year-round summer attracts visitors, especially those seeking refuge from snow and ice. Major American fast food chains have outlets in Jamaica, and supermarkets stock a wide range of American foods. In addition, cable TV and satellite dishes bring North America into the living rooms of a significant proportion of the population.

Sunshine Pizza

½-1 cup tomato sauce
¼ cup soft tofu
¼ tsp. salt
pinch garlic powder
pinch powdered hot pepper
4-6 whole wheat pita
1 sweet pepper, sliced in rings
1 cup mushrooms, sliced

1 small cucumber, sliced
1 small onion, thinly sliced
½ cup cooked corn, drained
¼ cup pineapple bits (opt.)
1 tsp. oregano
¼ tsp. basil
oil
olives

1. Preheat the oven to 400°F.

2. Blend the tomato sauce with the tofu, salt, garlic powder, and hot pepper.

3. Spread the pita with the tofu-tomato sauce.

4. Top with the pepper, mushrooms, cucumber, onion, corn, and pineapple.

5. Sprinkle with the oregano, basil, and a little oil. Decorate with olives.

6. Bake for 20 minutes, or until the vegetables are tender.

Serves

Per serving: Calories: 210, Protein: 8 gm., Fat: 1 gm., Carbohydrates: 39 gm.

Jamaican Style Veggy Burgers

2 cups cooked and drained
   gungo or pigeon peas
1 cup whole wheat bread
   crumbs
½ cup wheat germ
1 tsp. pickapeppa sauce
salt or tamari to taste
½ onion, grated
¼ tsp. coriander seeds

¼ tsp. cumin seeds
1 medium onion, finely chopped
1 clove garlic, crushed and
   chopped
¼ tsp. hot pepper, seeded and
   finely chopped
1 tsp. oil
whole wheat flour for coating
3 Tbsp. oil

1. Mash the peas slightly. Add the bread crumbs, wheat germ, pickapeppa sauce, and salt, and mix well.

2. In a heavy saucepan without oil, lightly brown the coriander and cumin seeds. Crush or grind the seeds.

3. Sauté the onion, garlic, and hot pepper in 1 tsp. oil until the onion is transparent.

4. Combine all the ingredients and form the mixture into 8 slightly flattened balls. Coat with the flour and fry in the oil on both sides until browned.

Serves 8

Per serving: Calories: 175, Protein: 7 gm., Fat: 7 gm., Carbohydrates: 21 gm.

Nyam Burgers

Nyam is a Jamaican creole word of African origin which means eat.

2 lbs. tofu, mashed
2 cups rolled oats or whole
   wheat bread crumbs
1 Tbsp. tamari
1 large onion, finely chopped
¼ tsp. fresh hot pepper,
   seeded and finely chopped

1 tsp. salt
½ cup celery, finely chopped
6 Tbsp. carrots, finely grated
flour and whole wheat bread
   crumbs for coating
oil for frying

1. In a bowl, combine all the ingredients except the bread crumbs and oil. Mix well and knead lightly until the mixture holds together well.

2. Form the mixture into flattened balls about 3 inches in diameter.

3. Roll in a mix of bread crumbs and flour, and fry in a skillet until the burgers are brown on both sides.

4. Serve hot on a burger bun or with sauce over boiled spaghetti or mashed potatoes.

Serves 6-8

Per serving: Calories: 210, Protein: 14 gm., Fat: 7 gm., Carbohydrates: 21 gm.

Cashew and Gungo Loaf

3 Tbsp. oil
1 large onion, finely chopped
1 clove garlic, crushed and
   chopped
¼ tsp. hot pepper, seeded and
   chopped
½ cup sweet pepper, seeded
   and chopped
1¼ cups soymilk or coconut
   milk
½ lb. tofu, or 2 eggs (lightly
   beaten), or egg replacer

1 cup cashews, finely chopped
2 cups whole wheat bread
   crumbs
2 cups cooked gungo peas or
  red kidney beans, mashed
1 tsp. dried thyme
1 tsp. salt
¼ cup fresh parsley, chopped
barbecue sauce (opt.)

1. Preheat the oven to 350°F.

2. Heat the oil in a small skillet and sauté the onion, garlic, hot pepper, and sweet pepper until the onion is transparent.

3. Blend the soymilk with the tofu until smooth.

4. Combine all the ingredients except the barbecue sauce.

5. Pack the mixture into an oiled 9 x 4-inch loaf pan.

6. Bake for 45 minutes. Serve with barbecue sauce, if you wish.

Serves 8

Per serving: Calories: 297, Protein: 11 gm., Fat: 16 gm., Carbohydrates: 27 gm.

Callalu Lasagna

12 oz. whole wheat lasagna
  noodles
½ lb. soft tofu
2-3 cups tomato sauce
1 medium onion, chopped
1 clove garlic, crushed
¼ tsp. hot pepper, seeded
  and chopped
½ lb. mushrooms, sliced
1 medium sweet pepper,
  seeded and chopped
1 lb. callalu or spinach

1 scallion, chopped
3 Tbsp. oil
1 pound tomatoes, skinned,
  seeded, and chopped
¼ tsp. dried thyme
¼ tsp. oregano
½ cup vegetable stock or
  soymilk
2 Tbsp. fresh parsley, chopped
salt to taste
½ cup whole wheat bread
  crumbs

1. Cook the lasagna in boiling water until the pasta is just tender, drain, and separate.

2. In a blender, purée the tofu and tomato sauce until smooth.

3. Sauté the onion, garlic, hot pepper, mushrooms, sweet pepper, callalu, and scallion in the oil. Add the tomatoes, thyme, oregano, and vegetable stock, and simmer until the callalu is tender and still green. Add the parsley and salt, and correct seasonings to taste.

4. Preheat the oven to 375°F.

5. Lightly grease a shallow baking dish, and place a layer of sauce at the base. Add a layer of pasta, and top with the callalu mixture. Repeat the process until the ingredients are all used, starting again with the sauce and ending with a layer of sauce.

6. Sprinkle with bread crumbs and bake for 30-40 minutes until the top is lightly browned. Let stand for 15 minutes, and serve.

Serves 10

Per serving: Calories: 250, Protein: 9 gm., Fat: 6 gm., Carbohydrates: 39 gm.

Sunday Macaroni Casserole

A macaroni casserole, traditionally macaroni and cheese, is frequently a part of the menu at a Sunday dinner.

12 oz. macaroni
1 cup Golden Sauce
   (page 111)
½ cup soft tofu
1 tsp. salt
¼ tsp. powdered hot pepper
¾ cup whole wheat bread
   crumbs
1 medium onion, chopped

1-2 cloves garlic, crushed and
   minced
½ cup mushrooms, sliced
½ cup sweet peppers, seeded
   and chopped
1 Tbsp. oil
¼ cup fresh parsley, chopped
¼ tsp. dried thyme

1. Cook the pasta until it is just tender, and drain.

2. Combine the Golden Sauce, tofu, salt, hot pepper, and half of the bread crumbs.

3. Preheat the oven to 375°F.

4. Sauté the onion, garlic, mushrooms, and sweet peppers in the oil until the onion is transparent.

5. Combine the pasta with the sauce and the seasonings, and add the parsley and thyme.

6. Put the mixture in a greased baking dish, sprinkle with the remaining bread crumbs, and bake for about 30 minutes until the top is light brown.

Serves 6

Per serving: Calories: 180, Protein: 5 gm., Fat: 8 gm., Carbohydrates: 22 gm.

Candied Sweet Potatoes

3 lbs. sweet potatoes
salted water
3 Tbsp. oil
1 cup brown sugar
1 tsp. molasses

½ cup honey
½ tsp. cinnamon
½ cup orange or pineapple juice
grated rind of 1 orange

1. Peel and cube the sweet potatoes, soak for 1-1½ hours in salted water, and drain.

2. Put the oil in a baking dish, and add the sweet potatoes.

3. Preheat the oven to 350°F.

4. Combine the sugar, molasses, honey, cinnamon, and orange juice and rind.

5. Sprinkle the liquid over the potatoes, and bake for 35-50 minutes until glazed and tender.

Serves 12

Per serving: Calories: 257, Protein: 2 gm., Fat: 4 gm., Carbohydrates: 56 gm.

Party Potato Salad

Potato salads are popular for festive occasions.

½ cup olive oil
¼ cup cider vinegar
1 tsp. salt
½ tsp. oregano
½ tsp. mustard powder
1 small clove garlic (opt.)
4 medium potatoes, cooked, peeled, and cubed
1 cup celery, chopped into ¼-inch pieces

1 medium onion, finely chopped
1 cup carrots, grated
1 green pepper, slivered
¼ tsp. hot pepper, seeded and finely chopped
2 Tbsp. fresh parsley, minced
2 scallions, finely chopped

1. Blend the oil, vinegar, salt, oregano, mustard powder, and garlic until smooth.

2. Pour over the hot potatoes, and marinate for at least an hour, or until the potatoes are cool.

3. Add the rest of the vegetables and the seasonings to the marinated potatoes.

4. Refrigerate for about 2 hours, and serve on a bed of lettuce.

Serves 6

Per serving: Calories: 265, Protein: 2 gm., Fat: 17 gm., Carbohydrates: 25 gm.

Garlic and Avocado Dressing

1 small, ripe avocado
1 Tbsp. lemon juice
⅛ tsp. salt
⅛ tsp. powdered hot pepper

1 tiny clove garlic, crushed
    and chopped
¼ cup soft tofu

Blend all the ingredients until smooth, and serve with a vegetable salad.

Tofu Mayonnaise

¼ cup lemon juice or cider
    vinegar
2 Tbsp. oil
1 tsp. salt
⅛ tsp. paprika

⅛ tsp. powdered hot pepper
pinch fresh garlic, crushed and
    minced
½ lb. soft tofu

1. Place all the ingredients in a blender, except for the tofu.

2. Add the tofu little by little, blending until the mixture is creamy smooth.

Makes about ⅓ cup

Per 2 Tbsp.: Calories: 35, Protein: 2 gm., Fat: 2 gm., Carbohydrates: 1 gm.

Variations: Add your favorite seasonings, tamari, or honey.

Piquant Tomato Sauce

1 medium onion, chopped
1 clove garlic
2 Tbsp. oil
1 small carrot, grated
1 sweet pepper, chopped
1 bay leaf
1 whole, unripe hot pepper
4 pimento grains (allspice)
2 scallions, crushed but not
   chopped

1 tsp. oregano
½ tsp. thyme
¼ tsp. basil
2 lbs. tomatoes, peeled, seeded,
   and chopped
2 Tbsp. fresh parsley, chopped
1 tsp. salt
¼ tsp. honey

1. Sauté the onion and garlic clove in the oil until the onion is transparent.

2. Add the carrot, sweet pepper, bay leaf, whole hot pepper, pimento grains (allspice), scallions, oregano, thyme, and basil.

3. Stir well and add the tomatoes, parsley, salt, and honey.

4. Simmer for about 30 minutes.

5. Remove the bay leaf, pimento grains (allspice), and scallions. Adjust the seasonings and purée in a blender until smooth.

Makes about 2 cups

Per ¼ cup: Calories: 67, Protein: 1 gm., Fat: 3 gm., Carbohydrates: 7 gm.

Brown Sauce

2 Tbsp. butter
2 Tbsp. whole wheat flour
1 cup vegetable stock

½ tsp. salt or tamari
herbs or spices to taste

1. Melt the butter in a saucepan.

2. Stir in the flour and cook for about 3 or 4 minutes, stirring constantly.

3. Add the vegetable stock slowly, always stirring.

4. Bring the sauce to a boil to thicken.

5. Add the herbs or spices, adjust the seasonings, and serve.

Makes 1 cup

Per ¼ cup: Calories: 67, Protein: 0 gm., Fat: 6 gm., Carbohydrates: 3 gm.

Golden Sauce

Follow the recipe for brown sauce, using unbleached flour instead of whole wheat flour, and using salt instead of tamari.

Dark Brown Sauce

Toast the flour in a dry pan, and then follow the recipe for brown sauce. Use tamari instead of salt.

Creamy Dip

1 lb. tofu
⅓ cup oil
1 Tbsp. lime juice or cider
  vinegar
1 Tbsp. tamari
1 clove garlic, crushed and
  finely minced

1 medium onion, finely chopped
dash hot pepper, seeded and
  minced
¼ cup fresh parsley, finely
  chopped
½ tsp. salt
1 Tbsp. honey

Place all the ingredients in a blender, and blend until smooth.

Makes 2½ cups

Per ¼ cup: Calories: 107, Protein: 3 gm., Fat: 8 gm., Carbohydrates: 4 gm.

GRANNY'S KITCHEN

A minority of Jamaicans eat exclusively vegetarian foods, but many items on the popular Jamaican menu are of plant origin. Slaves had limited rations of salted meat and were expected to provide for themselves from the produce of their vegetable gardens. Our grandmothers catered for their families without freezers, and so meat was available mainly on weekends. Granny's recipes were an amalgam of the cultures which she inherited and passed on. The dishes which she created—a little bit of this, a little bit of that, liberally seasoned with love and an insistence that you eat your belly full—contain memories that seem to thrive on foreign soil. Jamaican migrants have taken the essence of Granny's kitchen across the globe. Vegetarians are the beneficiaries of her limited use of meat.

Some special features of Granny's legacy are food rituals such as thick soup on Saturdays, rice and peas on Sundays, sorrel drink at Christmas time, and fruit drinks with all main meals.

A tradition of homemade drinks and candies exists that has been encouraged by the central role of the sugar cane industry in Jamaica's history. Raw sugar was usually used, with the vitamins and minerals not lost to refinement. Methods ranging from the simple to the esoteric are now being overtaken by sophistication in tastes and in technology. No longer evident are the vendors with glass cases displaying hard sweets called Paradise Plum, and also a mouth-watering confection of grated coconut and molasses, called by names such as Bus' Yuh Jaw, Stagga Back, and Bustamante Backbone.

Before our grandmothers had indoor kitchens, they made ice cream, cakes, and puddings. They produced all-natural ice cream (no preservatives!) in a hand-operated bucket freezer packed with ice which was bought by the block. The ice cream was usually made on Sunday afternoons and disappeared before nightfall. Cakes and puddings were baked in an outdoor coal stove with hot coals under and above the baking tin. These delicacies were referred to as "Hell on the top, Hell at the bottom, and Hallelujah in the middle."

Hospitality was then the convention, and drop-in guests were assured of a meal or at least a drink. Visitors to the home would traditionally be offered a cup of tea, if they arrived in the morning, or a cold beverage if they came later in the day.

Jugs of limeade, called wash or bebridge, continue to be on hand, especially during the hot summer months. Irish Moss, a gelatinous drink made from a seaweed, is still of special interest to males as it is credited with being an aphrodisiac.

Tea, in the context of Granny's kitchen, refers to a hot drink. Oriental tea is called green tea, and hot chocolate is called cocoa tea or chocolate tea. An herbal tea used for medicinal purposes is known as bush tea. Researchers from Jamaica and other parts of the world are increasingly finding a scientific basis for the intuitive knowledge of the Jamaican Granny. Scientific research on bush teas is not yet complete, and so prescribed dosages are not yet determined. Folk tradition credits these teas with aiding digestion (mint, gingerroot, and bissy), restoration of body temperature (lemon grass also called fever grass), internal cleansing and healing (cerasee, comfrey, search-me-heart), and male sexual performance (wood roots). Folk healing combined bush tea with a bush bath which was expected to cure ills of the body, mind, heart, and finances.

Vegetarian influences were strengthened by the East Indians who first arrived in Jamaica in 1845. They refrained from eating flesh altogether—for religious reasons—and were considered by the wider community as being eccentric eaters of greens.

The Seventh Day Adventists, a religious denomination, sought to alert its members to the dangers of eating animal foods if they were to enjoy a healthier, happier, holier life. Members of this group are pioneers in establishing business operations involved in producing, distributing, and providing outlets for vegetarian foods.

The Rastafarian faith also upholds ideals of vegetarianism. Salt is eliminated in foods which are termed ital. Rastafari originates in Jamaica, and supports the divinity of Ras Tafari, a title of Haile Selassie, the Emperor of Ethiopia. Some of the popular eating places in Kingston are operated by Rastafarians connected to such well-known names as Bob Marley and Mutabaruka.

The New Age movement has introduced many Jamaicans to the virtues of a life-style which is healthier, less toxic, and more environmentally friendly. Trends towards preventive health care and the conservation of the environment have also directed some Jamaicans towards vegetarianism.

Granny's kitchen is therefore traditional, representing the mixture of ethnic influences, and also modern, including current trends.

Bush Tea I

boiling water
tropical leaf or grass herb such
    as mint, lemon grass,
    comfrey, cerasee, or search-
    me-heart

honey or sugar to taste

1. Pour the boiling water over the tea leaves or grasses (about 1 cup of water for each teaspoon of tea).

2. Infuse for about 3 minutes, strain, and sweeten to taste.

Bush Tea II

tropical root herb such as
    gingerroot, sarsaparilla,
    chainey root, or bridal wiss

boiling water
honey or sugar to taste

1. Place the root in a saucepan of cold water (about ½ inch root for every cup of water.)

2. Bring to a boil and simmer for about 15 minutes.

3. Strain and sweeten to taste.

Bush Tea III

bissy (kola nut), grated　　　　**honey or sugar to taste**
boiling water

1. Pour the boiling water over the kola nut (about 1 tsp. kola nut for every cup of water).

2. Infuse for about 3 minutes, strain, and sweeten to taste.

Wash or Bebridge (Limeade)

4 Tbsp. lime juice　　　　**2 tsp. molasses (opt.)**
honey or sugar to taste　　**4 cups water**

Mix all the ingredients together, and serve with ice.

Serves 2

Per serving: Calories: 69, Protein: 0 gm., Fat: 0 gm., Carbohydrates: 17 gm.

Minty Limeade

Make the limeade and substitute 1 cup of cold mint tea for 1 cup of water.

Irish Moss Drink I

½ oz. Irish Moss (carrageenan)
   or agar-agar
4 cups water

¼ cup lime juice
honey or sugar to taste

1. Soak the Irish Moss for 3 hours or overnight.

2. Add the soaked Irish Moss to the water, bring to a boil, and simmer for 5 minutes.

3. Cool and strain the mixture. Add the lime juice and honey, and serve well chilled.

Serves 4

Per serving: Calories: 149, Protein: 1 gm., Fat: 0 gm., Carbohydrates: 35 gm.

Irish Moss Drink II

½ oz. Irish Moss (carrageenan)
   or agar-agar
4 cups soymilk
1 tsp. vanilla

¼ tsp. ground cinnamon
¼ tsp. ground nutmeg
honey or sugar to taste

1. Soak the Irish Moss for 3 hours or overnight.

2. Add the soaked Irish Moss to the soymilk, bring to a boil, and simmer for 5 minutes.

3. Cool and strain the mixture. Add the vanilla, cinnamon, nutmeg, and honey, and serve well chilled.

Serves 4

Per serving: Calories: 224, Protein: 6 gm., Fat: 5 gm., Carbohydrates: 39 gm.

Cucumber Drink

6 cups cucumbers, coarsely chopped
1 Tbsp. gingerroot, finely grated

6 cups water
1 Tbsp. lime juice
honey or sugar to taste

1. Blend the cucumbers, gingerroot, and water, and strain through a cloth.

2. Add the lime and honey, and serve chilled.

Serves 8

Per serving: Calories: 60, Protein: 0 gm., Fat: 0 gm., Carbohydrates: 14 gm.

Gingerroot Beer I

2 oz. gingerroot, peeled and grated
4 cups water

2 Tbsp. lime juice
peel of 1 lime, grated
about 1 cup honey or sugar

1. In a bowl, combine the gingerroot, water, lime juice, and lime peel, and stir well.

2. Leave covered for a day or overnight.

3. Strain the mixture, dilute if it is too strong, sweeten, and refrigerate. Serve well chilled or over ice.

Serves 4

Per serving: Calories: 272, Protein: 0 gm., Fat: 0 gm., Carbohydrates: 68 gm.

Gingerroot Beer II

6-8 oz. gingerroot, peeled and
   grated
1-2 oz. wood roots (opt.)
4-6 whole cloves (opt.)

½ lime or lemon, thinly sliced
16 cups boiling water
1 Tbsp. active dry yeast
about 4 cups honey

1. Combine the gingerroot, wood roots, cloves, and lime in a bowl. Pour the boiling water over the ingredients.

2. Dissolve the yeast in ¼ cup water which is at body temperature.

3. Allow the gingerroot mixture to become lukewarm, and then add the yeast mixture. Cover and set aside for a day or overnight to allow to ferment.

4. Strain the mixture, dilute if it is too strong, sweeten, and refrigerate. Serve well chilled or over ice.

Serves 16

Per serving: Calories: 271, Protein: 0 gm., Fat: 0 gm., Carbohydrates: 67 gm.

Fruit Punch

2 cups water
1 cup honey or brown sugar
4 cups pineapple juice
2 cups orange juice

1 cup grapefruit juice
1 cup guava juice
½ cup lime juice
2 cups cold gingerroot tea (opt.)

Mix all the ingredients together, adjust for sweetness or balance of flavors, and serve over ice.

Serves 10

Per serving: Calories: 210, Protein: 1 gm., Fat: 0 gm., Carbohydrates: 51 gm.

Lush Fruit Punch

1 cup water
½ cup honey or brown sugar
1 cup papaya, peeled, seeded,
    and cubed
4 slices pineapple, chopped

½ cup strawberries, chopped
1 orange, peeled and sectioned
    (preferably ortaniques)
¼ cup lime juice

Combine all the ingredients in a blender, and purée until smooth and creamy. Serve over ice.

Serves 4

Per serving: Calories: 198, Protein: 1 gm., Fat: 0 gm., Carbohydrates: 48 gm.

Pineapple Drink

about 1 Tbsp. gingerroot, grated
1 whole clove (opt.)
peelings from 1 pineapple

about 2 inches dried orange peel
4 cups boiling water
brown sugar or honey to taste

1. Place the gingerroot, clove, pineapple, and orange peel in a glass bowl, and pour on the boiling water.

2. Cover and leave to steep overnight.

3. Strain, sweeten, and serve well chilled or over ice.

Serves 4

Per serving: Calories: 66, Protein: 0 gm., Fat: o gm., Carbohydrates: 6 gm.

Passion Fruit Drink

8-12 passion fruits
about 5 cups water
½ cup lime juice

1 cup ortanique juice (opt.)
honey to taste

1. Cut the passion fruits and put the pulp and seeds in a container.

2. Add the remaining ingredients and mix thoroughly. Strain, dilute if necessary, and serve chilled or over ice.

Serves 5

Per serving: Calories: 196, Protein: 1 gm., Fat: 0 gm., Carbohydrates: 46 gm.

Mango Drink

6 ripe mangoes, peeled, seeded, and diced
2 cups water

¼ cup lime juice
brown sugar or honey to taste

1. Combine the mangoes, water, and lime juice in a blender, and purée until smooth.

2. Strain if mango fibres remain, sweeten, and serve well-chilled or over ice.

Serves 6

Per serving: Calories: 172, Protein: 1 gm., Fat: 0 gm., Carbohydrates: 41 gm.

Tamarind Drink

3 cups tamarinds, shelled
1 tsp. gingerroot, chopped

6 cups water
2 cups honey or sugar

1. Soak the tamarinds and gingerroot in the water for 2 hours or overnight.

2. Use a wooden spoon to rub the tamarind seeds against the sides of the bowl until the pulp is removed, and strain.

3. Sweeten the mixture, diluting if necessary. Refrigerate and serve chilled or over ice.

Serves 6

Per serving: Calories: 357, Protein: 0 gm., Fat: 0 gm., Carbohydrates: 90 gm.

Garden Cherry Drink

2 cups garden cherries   **honey to taste**
about 1½ cups water

1. Wash the cherries and place in a blender with water. Blend for a count of about twenty, or until the pulp is released but the seeds are not yet crushed.

2. Rub the mixture through a sieve, dilute as necessary, and sweeten. Serve chilled or over ice.

Serves 3-4

Per serving: Calories: 118, Protein: 1 gm., Fat: 0 gm., Carbohydrates: 29 gm.

Carrot Drink

1 lb. small fresh carrots, finely   **½ cup lime juice**
grated   **honey or brown sugar to taste**
4 cups water

1. In a blender, combine the carrots and water, and blend thoroughly.

2. Strain the mixture, dilute if necessary, and add the lime juice and honey. Serve well chilled or over ice.

Serves 6

Per serving: Calories: 125, Protein: 1 gm., Fat: 0 gm., Carbohydrates: 31 gm.

Creamy Carrot Drink

1 lb. small fresh carrots, finely grated
4 cups soymilk
¼ tsp. nutmeg

¼ tsp. cinnamon
½ tsp. vanilla
honey to taste

1. In a blender, combine the carrots and soymilk, and blend thoroughly.

2. Strain the mixture, dilute if necessary, and add the nutmeg, cinnamon, and vanilla. Sweeten and serve well chilled or over ice.

Note: You can substitute steamed mashed carrots for the fresh grated carrots.

Serves 6

Per serving (using 4 Tbsp. honey): Calories: 129, Protein: 4 gm., Fat: 3 gm., Carbohydrates: 21 gm.

Carrot and Beet Drink

½ lb. small fresh carrots, washed and scraped
½ lb. beets, washed and peeled

4 cups water
½ cup lime juice
½ cup orange juice
honey to taste

1. Cut the carrots and beets into cubes, combine in a blender with the water, and blend thoroughly.

2. Strain the mixture, dilute if necessary, and sweeten. Serve chilled or over ice.

Serves 6-8

Per serving: Calories: 111, Protein: 1 gm., Fat: 0 gm., Carbohydrates: 27 gm.

Pumpkin Drink

1 lb. pumpkin, steamed and
    cubed
4 cups soymilk
¼ tsp. nutmeg

¼ tsp. cinnamon
½ tsp. vanilla
honey to taste

1. Mash the pumpkin and combine with the soymilk.

2. Strain the mixture, dilute if necessary, and add the nutmeg, cinnamon, and vanilla. Sweeten and serve well chilled or over ice.

Serves 4

Per serving: Calories: 182, Protein: 6 gm., Fat: 5 gm., Carbohydrates: 29 gm.

Peanut Punch

½ cup smooth peanut butter
About 2 cups soymilk or
    coconut milk

½ tsp. vanilla
½ tsp. cinnamon
brown sugar or honey to taste

Blend the peanut butter, soymilk, vanilla, and cinnamon in a blender until the mixture is smooth. Sweeten to taste and serve well chilled or over ice.

Serves 4

Per serving: Calories: 261, Protein: 10 gm., Fat: 17 gm., Carbohydrates: 18 gm.

Sorrel Drink

2-3 ounces dried sorrel
1 oz. gingerroot, peeled and
   grated
6 cloves
8 pimento grains (allspice)

2 quarts boiling water
about 2 cups brown sugar or
   honey
½ -1 cup white rum (opt.)

1. Place the sorrel, gingerroot, cloves, and pimento grains (allspice) in a large bowl.

2. Cover with the boiling water, and leave to steep overnight.

3. Strain, sweeten to taste, add rum if you choose. Bottle, chill well, and serve over ice.

Serves 6-8

Per serving: Calories: 184, Protein: 0 gm., Fat: 0 gm., Carbohydrates: 46 gm.

Fruit Snow

3 cups crushed ice
2 cups mangoes or papaya,
   peeled, seeded, and diced

¼ cup honey or sugar
1 Tbsp. lime or lemon juice
sprigs of mint or slices of lime or
   lemon

1. In a blender, combine the ice, mangoes, honey, and lime juice, and blend until the mixture is slushy.

2. Pour into glasses, garnish with mint leaves or lime slices, and serve immediately.

Serves 6

Per serving: Calories: 80, Protein: 0 gm., Fat: 0 gm., Carbohydrates: 20 gm.

Banana Yogurt Drink

2 cups plain yogurt
¼ tsp. cinnamon

2 ripe bananas, chopped just before using
2 tsp. lime juice

Combine all the ingredients in a blender, and purée until smooth. Serve well chilled or over crushed ice.

Serves 3-4

Per serving: Calories: 147, Protein: 6 gm., Fat: 4 gm., Carbohydrates: 20 gm.

Icy Pops

4 cups unsweetened fruit juice
¼ cup lime or lemon juice

honey to taste
ice-trays and icicle sticks

1. Combine the fruit juices and honey.

2. Pour the liquid into the ice trays, and insert the icicle sticks.

3. Leave to harden in the freezer.

Serves 4

Per serving: Calories: 57, Protein: 1 gm., Fat: 0 gm., Carbohydrates: 13 gm.

Hominy Porridge

½ cup hominy corn, or
   cracked corn
6 cups water
2 cinnamon sticks
1 piece mace (the outside fibre
   of a nutmeg)

¼ tsp. salt
⅓ cup whole wheat flour
2 cups coconut milk
1 tsp. grated nutmeg
½ tsp. vanilla
1 cup soymilk

1. Soak the corn in the water overnight.

2. Place the corn, the water in which it has been soaked, the cinnamon sticks, mace, and salt in a saucepan.

3. Bring to a boil and simmer for 1½ hours.

4. Mix the flour with a little coconut milk to form a smooth paste, then add the rest of the coconut milk to the paste.

5. Add the paste mixture to the saucepan, stir well, and bring the porridge back to a boil.

6. Add the nutmeg, vanilla, and soymilk. Cook for about 10 minutes more, and serve hot.

Serves 6-8

Per serving: Calories: 267, Protein: 4 gm., Fat: 15 gm., Carbohydrates: 25 gm.

Festival

1 cup whole wheat flour
1 cup cornmeal
pinch salt
¼ tsp. allspice
¼ tsp. baking soda
1 Tbsp. honey or brown sugar

¼ tsp. rose water
¼ tsp. vanilla
about ½ cup soymilk or water
3 Tbsp. flour
1 Tbsp. cornmeal
oil for frying

1. Sift together 1 cup whole wheat flour, 1 cup cornmeal, salt, allspice, and baking soda.

2. Add the honey, rose water, and vanilla to the soymilk.

3. Add the liquid to the dry ingredients, knead lightly, and leave covered for 30 minutes.

4. Divide the dough into 10-12 portions.

5. Knead lightly, then roll and pull each portion to form a flattened sausage shape 4-6 inches long x 1½ inches diameter.

6. Mix together 3 Tbsp. flour and 1 Tbsp. cornmeal.

7. Dip the dough in the flour and cornmeal mixture. Fry the Festival in hot oil until the it is golden-brown on the outside and cooked on the inside.

8. Serve with Escabeche Tofu (page 45), Jerked Tofu (page 38), or fried Nyam Burgers (page 103) or Jamaican Style Veggy Burgers (page 102).

Serves 6-7

Per serving: Calories: 171, Protein: 5 gm., Fat: 1 gm., Carbohydrates: 36 gm.

Rice and Peas

1 cup dried red peas
2 cloves garlic, crushed
3 cups water
milk from 1 dried coconut
salt to taste
¼ tsp. hot pepper, seeded and chopped

2 scallions, crushed
¼ tsp. dried thyme
2 cups brown rice
1 whole, unripe hot pepper
6 pimento grains (allspice)
2 bay leaves

1. Wash the peas and soak overnight in enough water to cover. Drain and rinse.

2. Combine the peas, garlic, water, coconut milk, and salt. Bring to a boil and simmer for about 2 hours until the peas are cooked but firm.

3. Add the chopped hot pepper, scallions, and thyme. Then add the rice, whole hot pepper, pimento grains (allspice), bay leaves, and as much water as needed to cook the rice.

4. Return to a boil, reduce the heat, and simmer for about 45 minutes, or until the rice is cooked. Serve hot.

Serves 6-8

Per serving: Calories: 288, Protein: 7 gm., Fat: 8 gm., Carbohydrates: 44 gm.

Peppered Gluten Steak

½ Tbsp. gingerroot, finely chopped
3 scallions, chopped
3 cloves garlic, finely chopped
¼ tsp. dried thyme
1 medium onion, sliced
1 Tbsp. tamari
salt to taste

1½ lbs. gluten (fresh or canned)
2 Tbsp. oil
1 cup sweet pepper, julienned
1 Tbsp. cornstarch
1½ cups water
1 Tbsp. pickapeppa sauce (opt.)

1. Make a marinade of the gingerroot, scallions, garlic, thyme, onion, tamari, and salt. Pour over the gluten and let to marinate for 2 hours.

2. Heat the oil, sauté the sweet pepper, and remove it from the frying pan.

3. Remove the gluten from the marinade, and fry it until it is a deeper brown color.

4. Return the sweet pepper to the pan, and add the marinade.

5. Combine the cornstarch with 2 Tbsp. of the water, then add it to the pan with the remainder of the water, and the pickapeppa sauce.

6. Stir until the sauce thickens, and serve hot with plain rice, rice and peas, or mashed potatoes.

Serves 6

Per serving: Calories: 244, Protein: 39 gm., Fat: 5 gm., Carbohydrates: 10 gm.

Rasta Pasta

1 lb. macaroni
2 cloves garlic, crushed and
    chopped
2 scallions, chopped
½ cup red sweet peppers,
    julienned
1 medium onion, chopped
1 Tbsp. oil
¼ tsp. each: thyme and basil

¼ tsp. hot pepper, seeded and
    chopped
1 cup cooked corn kernels
1 cup broccoli, broken into
    florets and lightly steamed
½ cup fresh parsley, chopped
about 1 quart of sauce,
    preferably tomato

1. Cook the macaroni until firm and tender. Drain and place on a serving dish.

2. Sauté the garlic, scallions, sweet peppers, and onion in the oil until the onion is transparent.

3. Add the thyme, basil, hot pepper, corn, broccoli, parsley, and sauce, and heat fully.

4. Pour the sauce mixture over the macaroni, and serve hot.

Serves 6

Per serving: Calories: 192, Protein: 5 gm., Fat: 3 gm., Carbohydrates: 36 gm.

Pumpkin Sauce

2 scallions, chopped
1 clove garlic, crushed and
   chopped
¼ tsp. fresh hot pepper,
   seeded and chopped
1 tsp. oil
½ lb. pumpkin, steamed and
   cubed

½ cup water from the steamed
   pumpkin
salt to taste
1 tsp. cornstarch (opt.)
fresh parsley for garnishing,
   chopped

1. In a heavy saucepan, lightly sauté the scallions, garlic, and hot pepper in the oil, and stir in the pumpkin cubes.

2. Place the pumpkin mixture and water from the steamed pumpkin in a food processor or blender, and blend until smooth.

3. Return the mixture to the saucepan, add the salt, and reheat.

4. Make a paste of the cornstarch, and add this to the mixture if you want a thick sauce.

5. Garnish with parsley and serve.

Serves 4

Per serving: Calories: 34, Protein: 0 gm., Fat: 1 gm., Carbohydrates: 5 gm.

Toto

1½ cups flour
1½ tsp. baking powder
½ tsp. baking soda
½ tsp. mixed spice
½ cup brown sugar
¼ cup honey

¼ cup molasses
2 oz. butter or margarine
¼ cup soymilk
2 oz. soft tofu, or 1 egg or egg
  replacer
1 cup grated coconut

1. Preheat the oven to 300°F.

2. Sift the dry ingredients.

3. Blend the honey, molasses, butter, soymilk, and tofu.

4. Add the liquid to the dry ingredients, beat well, and stir in the coconut.

5. Bake for 1 hour, cool, and cut into squares.

Serves 12

Per serving: Calories: 261, Protein: 3 gm., Fat: 16 gm., Carbohydrates: 27 gm.

Jackass Corn

1 cup flour
¼ tsp. each: grated nutmeg,
   cinnamon, and salt

¼ tsp. baking soda
⅔ cup brown sugar
1¼ cups grated coconut

1. Preheat the oven to 375°F.

2. Sift the dry ingredients and combine with the brown sugar.

3. Place the coconut in a bowl, and add the dry ingredients. Work the ingredients together until a dough is formed.

4. Roll out the dough until it is as thin as paper. Cut into 2-inch circles or squares.

5. Bake on a greased cookie tin for 10-12 minutes or until light brown. Store, when cool, in an airtight tin.

Serves 25-30

Per serving: Calories: 94, Protein: 1 gm., Fat: 6 gm., Carbohydrates: 8 gm.

Bulla

4 cups whole wheat flour
1 tsp. baking powder
½ tsp. baking soda
¼ tsp. salt
1 Tbsp. ground ginger

½ tsp. cinnamon
½ cup water
1 cup honey or brown sugar
1 Tbsp. molasses
2 Tbsp. oil

1. Preheat the oven to 375°F.

2. Sift all the dry ingredients into a bowl.

3. Combine the water, molasses, and oil.

4. Add the liquid to the dry ingredients to form a soft dough.

5. Knead the dough for a few minutes on a lightly floured board. Roll out about ½ inch thick and cut into 3-inch rounds.

6. Place on a baking tray that has been greased and floured, and bake for about 20 minutes or until done.

Serves 24

Per serving: Calories: 123, Protein: 3 gm., Fat: 2 gm., Carbohydrates: 25 gm.

Sweet Potato Pudding

1½ lbs. sweet potatoes,
  grated
2 oz. yellow yams, grated
  (opt.)
3 cups coconut milk, or 2 cups
  soymilk and 1 cup coconut
  cream
1 cup honey or brown sugar
1 Tbsp. molasses (opt.)
1 tsp. ground ginger

1 tsp. grated nutmeg
½ tsp. grated cinnamon
½ cup whole wheat flour
1 cup grated coconut (opt.)
1 tsp. vanilla
½ tsp. almond flavoring
½ cup raisins
¼ cup currants
2 Tbsp. coconut oil (opt.)
2 Tbsp. honey (opt.)

1. Preheat the oven to 350°F.

2. Combine the sweet potatoes, yams, coconut milk, honey, molasses, spices, and flour, and mix well.

3. Add the coconut, vanilla, almond flavoring, raisins, and currants, and pour the batter into a well-greased 8-inch baking tin or dish. Sprinkle the top with a mixture of coconut oil and honey.

4. Bake for 1-1½ hours until a skewer inserted in the pudding comes out clean. The pudding will become firmer as it cools. Serve hot or cold.

Serves 16

Per serving: Calories: 221, Protein: 2 gm., Fat: 6 gm., Carbohydrates: 38 gm.

Cornmeal Pudding

3 cups cornmeal
½ cup whole wheat flour
6 cups soymilk or coconut milk
2 cups honey or brown sugar
½ tsp. ground cinnamon
½ tsp. ground nutmeg

2 tsp. vanilla
½ tsp. almond flavoring
1 cup raisins
½ cup currants
2 Tbsp. coconut oil (opt.)
2 Tbsp. honey

1. Preheat the oven to 300°F.

2. Combine the cornmeal and whole wheat flour. Add the soymilk gradually, and mix until the batter is smooth.

3. Stir in the honey, spices, vanilla, almond flavoring, raisins, and currants.

4. Pour the batter into a greased baking dish or tin, and sprinkle the top with a mixture of oil and honey.

5. Bake for 1½ hours until a skewer inserted into the pudding comes out clean. The pudding will become firmer as it cools. Serve hot or cold.

Serves 12

Per serving: Calories: 418, Protein: 7 gm., Fat: 3 gm., Carbohydrates: 91 gm.

Christmas Cake

½ cup mixed, dried tropical
    fruit (papaya, carambola,
    pineapple, otaheite apple)
1 cup raisins
1 cup currants
1 cup prunes, stoned
about 2 cups grape juice
1 lb. soft tofu, mashed
6 ripe bananas, mashed
2 Tbsp. lime or lemon juice
grated rind of 2 limes or
    lemons
¼ cup mixed peel
1 tsp. vanilla

½ tsp. almond flavoring
½ cup honey
1 cup oil
4 cups unbleached or whole
    wheat flour
3 tsp. baking powder
1 tsp. cinnamon
1 tsp. nutmeg
½ tsp. ginger
1 cup whole wheat bread crumbs
1 cup carrots, grated
½ cup grated coconut (opt.)
½ cup unsalted cashew nuts,
    chopped (opt.)

1. Preheat the oven to 250°F.

2. Place the dried fruit, raisins, currants, and prunes in a saucepan with the grape juice, and steam the fruit until the raisins fill out.

3. Chop the fruit in a blender or food processor, and set aside to cool.

4. In a blender, combine the tofu, bananas, lime juice, lime rind, mixed peel, vanilla, almond flavoring, honey, and oil, and blend until the mixture is smooth.

5. Sift together the flour and baking powder. Add the spices and bread crumbs.

6. Add the puréed ingredients to the dry ingredients. Mix lightly and thoroughly.

7. Fold in the dried fruit, carrots, coconut, and cashews.

8. Pour the batter into a lined and well-greased 12-inch cake tin, or into smaller tins of equivalent volume.

9. Bake for about 2-3 hours until a skewer inserted into the middle of the cake comes out clean. Cool in the tin for about 5 minutes, then remove and cool on a rack.

Christmas Pudding

Follow the recipe for Christmas Cake, and place a bowl of water at the bottom of the oven during the baking process.

Serves 24

Per serving: Calories: 293, Protein: 4 gm., Fat: 10 gm., Carbohydrates: 46 gm.

Cut Cake (Coconut Drops)

2 cups diced coconut   **2½ cups brown sugar**
1 Tbsp. gingerroot, grated

1. In a heavy saucepan, cover the coconut with water.

2. Simmer until the coconut is tender, about 15 minutes to 2 hours. Add more water, if required.

3. Gradually add the sugar, and boil for about 15 minutes until the mixture forms a hard ball if a drop is placed in cold water.

4. Drop, tablespoon by tablespoon, on a damp cookie sheet, and leave to set.

Makes 40 pieces

Per piece: Calories: 109, Protein: 1 gm., Fat: 6 gm., Carbohydrates: 10 gm.

Honey Grater Cake

3 cups brown sugar
½ cup water

2 cups grated coconut

1. Heat the brown sugar and water in a heavy saucepan.

2. Add the coconut and boil, stirring constantly until the mixture is thick. A little of the mixture should form a ball if dropped into cold water.

3. Remove from the heat and beat for about 3 minutes.

4. Drop by spoonfuls onto a greased cookie sheet, and let set.

Serves 40

Per serving: Calories: 127, Protein: 1 gm., Fat: 6 gm., Carbohydrates: 15 gm.

Mango Cheese

4 cups mango pulp
3 cups brown sugar

peel of 1 lime
2 tsp. lime juice

1. Place all the ingredients in a heavy saucepan.

2. Bring to a boil and continue to boil rapidly, stirring constantly with a wooden spoon.

3. Cook for about 30 minutes, or until the mixture comes away from the sides of the pan. Remove the lime peel.

4. Pour the mixture into an 8-inch-square tin. Let set then cut in squares.

Serves 16

Per serving: Calories: 181, Protein: 0 gm., Fat: 0 gm., Carbohydrates: 44 gm.

Guava Cheese

4 cups guava pulp
4 cups brown sugar

peel of 1 lime
2 tsp. lime juice

1. Follow the Mango Cheese recipe.

Serves 16

Per serving: Calories: 226, Protein: 0 gm., Fat: 0 gm., Carbohydrates: 55 gm.

Bustamante Backbone

1¼ cups molasses
¼ cup water
peel of 1 lime
1 small stick of cinnamon
1 small piece mace

2 Tbsp. gingerroot, grated
3 cups grated coconut, coconut chips, or coconut trash from which the milk has been squeezed

1. Combine the molasses, water, lime peel, cinnamon, mace, and gingerroot in a heavy saucepan.

2. Cook until the syrup spins a thread from a spoon dipped in the mixture.

3. Remove the mixture from the stove. Take out the lime peel, cinnamon, and mace, and stir in the coconut. Beat until the mixture is thick.

4. Drop by spoonfuls on a greased cookie sheet, and allow to set.

Serves 40

Per serving: Calories: 147, Protein: 1 gm., Fat: 11 gm., Carbohydrates: 12 gm.

Peanut Brittle

2 cups chopped peanuts   **2 cups brown sugar**

1. Place the peanuts at the bottom of an 8-inch-square tin.

2. Melt the sugar in a heavy saucepan, and stir constantly until the sugar becomes caramel.

3. Pour the caramel over the peanuts immediately, and leave to set.

4. Cut into squares when almost set, or break into pieces after the mixture is set.

Serves 16

Per serving: Calories: 209, Protein: 4 gm., Fat: 8 gm., Carbohydrates: 29 gm.

Coconut Fudge

2 cups coconut milk
2 cups brown sugar

1 tsp. vanilla
½ tsp. ground cinnamon

1. Combine all the ingredients in a heavy saucepan over medium heat. Bring to a boil, stirring all the time.

2. Lower the heat and continue to boil the mixture until it thickens, stirring constantly.

3. Remove the mixture from the heat when sugar crystals form on the side of the pan.

4. Beat the mixture for a few minutes, and pour into a greased dish about 2 inches deep.

5. Allow to cool and when still warm, cut into squares.

Serves 16

Per serving: Calories: 173, Protein: 1 gm., Fat: 6 gm., Carbohydrates: 28 gm.

Mango Ice Cream

2 lbs. soft tofu
1 cup soymilk
1⅓ cups honey or sugar
1 cup oil
¼ cup lime or lemon juice

1 tsp. almond flavoring
1 tsp. vanilla flavoring
2 cups mangos, peeled, seeded,
    and cubed

1. Blend all the ingredients in a blender or food processor until the mixture is smooth and creamy.

2. Freeze in an ice cream maker, and serve in chilled dessert dishes.

Serves 6-8

Per serving: Calories: 615, Protein: 10 gm., Fat: 36 gm., Carbohydrates: 60 gm.

Coconut Ice Cream

2 lbs. soft tofu
1 cup coconut milk
1⅓ cups honey or sugar

1 cup oil
¼ cup lime or lemon juice
1 Tbsp. vanilla

1. Blend all the ingredients in a blender or food processor until the mixture is smooth and creamy.

2. Freeze in an ice cream maker, and serve in chilled dessert dishes.

Serves 8

Per serving: Calories: 571, Protein: 8 gm., Fat: 37 gm., Carbohydrates: 47 gm.

Fruit and Nut Ice Cream

1 lb. soft tofu
2 cups soymilk
¾ cup oil
⅔ cup honey or sugar
3 ripe bananas
1 cup papaya, peeled,
    seeded, and chopped

2 Tbsp. vanilla
pinch salt
¼ cup raisins
¼ cup cashews, chopped

1. Blend the tofu, soymilk, oil, honey, bananas, papaya, vanilla, and salt in a blender or food processor until the mixture is smooth and creamy.

2. Add the raisins and cashews.

3. Freeze in an ice cream maker, and serve in chilled dessert dishes.

Serves 6-8

Per serving: Calories: 475, Protein: 8 gm., Fat: 29 gm., Carbohydrates: 45 gm.

Fruit Salad

3 ripe bananas, peeled and
  sliced
2 ripe mangoes, peeled,
  seeded, and sliced
1 small ripe papaya, peeled,
  seeded, and cubed

1 small fresh pineapple, peeled,
  cored, and cubed
2 oranges, peeled and sectioned
  (preferably ortaniques)
½ cup strawberries, halved
1-2 cups guava juice

1. Combine all the ingredients in a salad bowl.

2. Chill for about 4 hours, and serve.

Serves 6-8

Per serving: Calories: 127, Protein: 1 gm., Fat: 0 gm., Carbohydrates: 29 gm.

Index

Ask your bookstore to carry these books, or you may order directly from:

The Book Publishing Company
P.O. Box 99
Summertown, TN 38483
1-800-695-2241

Please add $3.00 per book for shipping

Flavors of India
$12.95

Flavors of Korea
$12.95

A Taste of Mexico
$14.95

Flavors of the Southwest
$12.95

Nonna's Italian Kitchen
$14.95

Good Time Eatin' in Cajun Country
$9.95

Japanese Cooking
$12.95

From the Tables of Lebanon
$12.95

From a Traditional Greek Kitchen
$12.95

Cookin' Southern
$12.95

Pasta East to West
$14.95

Chili!
$12.95

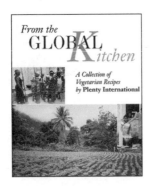

From the Global Kitchen
$11.95

Authentic Chinese Cuisine!
$12.95